Seven Days
for Ruby

Books by Blaine M. Yorgason and/or Brenton G. Yorgason

Seven Days for Ruby
Family Knights****
Pardners
The Eleven-Dollar Surgery
Bfpstk and the Smile Song***
The Shadow Taker**
The Loftier Way: Tales from the Ancient American Frontier
Brother Brigham's Gold
Ride the Laughing Wind
The Miracle
Chester, I Love You (paperback—movie version)
Chester, I Love You
Double Exposure
Seeker of the Gentle Heart
The Krystal Promise
A Town Called Charity, and Other Stories About Decisions
The Bishop's Horse Race
The Courage Covenant (Massacre at Salt Creek)
Windwalker (movie version—out of print)
The Windwalker
Others
Charlie's Monument
From First Date to Chosen Mate
Tall Timber (out of print)
Miracles and the Latter-day Saint Teenager (out of print)
From Two to One*
From This Day Forth*
Creating a Celestial Marriage (textbook)*
Marriage and Family Stewardships (textbook)*

Tapes

Caring and Sharing (Blaine M. Yorgason—two taped talks)
Things Most Plain and Precious (Brenton G. Yorgason—two taped talks)
The Joyous Way (Blaine & Brenton Yorgason—two taped talks)
Rhinestones and Rubies (Brenton G. Yorgason—two taped talks)
The Miracle (dramatized tape of book)
Charlie's Monument (taped reading of book)
The Bishop's Horse Race (taped reading of book)

*Coauthored with Wesley R. Burr and Terry R. Baker
**Coauthored with Carl J. Eaton
***Coauthored with Tami B. Yorgason
****Coauthored with Margaret Yorgason

Seven Days
for Ruby

Blaine M. Yorgason
Brenton G. Yorgason

Deseret Book Company
Salt Lake City, Utah

ISBN 0-87579-066-6
Library of Congress Catalog Card Number 86-72357

First printing November 1986

For Dick and Sharleen, and for Jim and Analee

Contents

Acknowledgments

We would like to acknowledge the invaluable help of Cora Beck Adamson and Stephen F. Beck, who recorded their histories as they unfolded.

Prologue

Saturday

October 1, 1910

The sun beat mercilessly against the concrete of the Los Angeles street, and the passersby walked faster, hoping to get more quickly into the coolness of their destinations. The street was not crowded, for it was Saturday. Neither was it empty. Yet the scattered pedestrians paid almost no attention to each other, all hurrying along on their own predetermined errands.

An automobile horn blared at an intersection, from down the street another answered, and two carriages passed around each other, the hooves of their teams clattering loudly against the pavement. A freight team dragged its creaking wagon slowly through the intersection, blocking the way of yet another motorcar. Overhead, a maze of telephone, telegraph, and electrical wires swung between poles, and the quiet buzzing from some of them added to the din of the street.

Fifty feet west of the intersection, a solitary man leaned against the front of a cafe, a copy of the *American Fork Citizen* folded neatly in his hand. His face and clothing were dark, and his white shirt showed more patches of dirt than of white. He was of indeterminate age, though his gray hair made him look more old than young. Between his teeth burned a large cigar, and every few seconds he puffed the red end aglow, expelling the smoke from the side of his mouth.

Suddenly the street was filled with the clatter of an engine, and seconds later a second man, riding an Indian motorcycle, pulled up to the curb across the street. He was dressed like the first and looked strangely similar. The difference was that he was younger, quite a bit younger.

For a long breath the second man leaned against his bike in front of the office of the *Los Angeles Times,* looking around. Then, as though he were ashamed of what he was about to do, he dropped his head and eyes. Next he lifted a bundle of newspapers from the front of the motorcycle and furtively carried them into the newspaper office, his eyes never once lifting from the sidewalk.

A moment later the man reappeared, climbed back on the motorcycle, glanced briefly in the direction of the man who still leaned against the cafe, and then roared off down the street.

For several minutes nothing else happened. Then, slowly, the remaining man looked up and read the sign that hung above him.

CHOICE FRUITS
CANDIES
CIGARETTES
HOT FRANKFURTERS
2¢ each

Satisfied that the sign had not changed since he had read it moments earlier, the man puffed again on his cigar, pushed away from the cafe wall, and limped slowly across the street. Then he pushed his way through the door of the newspaper offices, stopped, and looked around.

There were more people in the office than he had expected, several more. In fact, he had been led to believe that the office would be almost empty. It wasn't, and the street held more traffic than he had anticipated, too. But such things hardly mattered. Maybe, he thought, grinning, it would make the deal better than ever.

Casually he moved to the counter and saw that the clerk was busy. And so, as a waiting man might, he glanced at his feet. A stack of newspapers rested there, old papers, and he gingerly stooped down to leaf through them.

A long article caught his attention, and like a man deep in thought, he took the cigar from his mouth, held it between his fingers, and continued to read.

The ash built up. He subconsciously flicked it onto the floor, and as he brought the cigar back, the burning end touched a thick, black string that twisted out of the stack of paper at his feet. There the cigar held.

For an instant nothing happened, and the man glanced down. But with nerves of steel he held the cigar steady as he began again to read. Finally, with a sputter, the string or fuse caught fire.

Casually the man dropped the paper back onto the stack, where it covered the spitting fuse. Without hurry, then, he smiled at the young woman who was so busy behind the counter, nodded politely at a man who stood with her, and started for the door. A moment later he tipped his hat to an elderly woman who had come in, held the door open for a newsboy who seemed in a hurry to leave, and then passed outside.

Scant seconds afterward, with no warning, the stack of old papers, hollowed out and containing eight sticks of Du Pont Superior Brand dynamite, exploded in a ball of red and yellow flame. The fire rose to the thin ceiling and billowed on upward and outward, burning, consuming. The explosion blasted out windows a city block away, blew down walls in several adjoining buildings, killed twenty people who had the misfortune of being nearby, and, of course, stopped the presses.

And in the screaming melee that followed, no one saw the older man limping quietly away, a twisted smile of grim satisfaction on his face.

Day 1

Friday
October 21, 1910

Chapter 1

Ruby Soderberg Alder was fit to be tied. She had been up half the night and most of the morning waiting, and yet nothing had happened. Still, something was going to happen, she just knew it was. Not good, necessarily, nor bad—but *something*.

For the hundredth time she looked out the window, scanning her horizons, searching for something, anything . . .

It had been a beautiful October morning. Earlier the frost had blanketed everything, and then the sun had come up and the air had been crisp and bright and clear. Quickly the sun had melted the frost, and everything had been damp and clean-looking. It had been one of those mornings when nothing could have been more perfect than it already was.

Except that something unusual was going to happen, and Ruby knew it.

She had experienced that same feeling before, perhaps two dozen times in her seventy years of life. And not once had she ever been wrong. A few times it hadn't been quite so strong a feeling as she was having now, but always it had been *something*. And so she believed this feeling with all her heart.

The last time had been when her son had been called as bishop of their ward down in American Fork. She had known that blessed event was coming for two full days. Not precisely, of course, but something . . . something . . .

Another time had been when her milk cow had birthed a two-headed calf. She'd thought it a disaster until her nephew Hyrum Soderberg had sold it to a traveling gypsy show for twenty-five dollars. That money had come in handy, and so the something had turned out good. But good or bad, Ruby had known *something* was coming for almost an entire week before that calf was born.

Just like now, she thought as she moved the needle back on her new talking machine so that the music would start over. Something was going to happen, and she could hardly contain her anticipation.

Drying the last dish and putting it in the cupboard, she was dancing gaily to the music when through her kitchen window she saw the old man.

And instantly, she knew that the *something* she had expected was there.

Anxiously she watched the old man's steady approach, noting his limp, his slightly stooped shoulders, his tattered overalls, the shock of white hair that seemed to peek out from beneath the brim of his battered old hat. But mostly she watched his face, noticing that he looked neither to the right nor to the left but kept his gaze fixed upon the small house wherein she stood. Nor did he hurry. He just kept coming slowly forward, and Ruby felt her throat constrict as she watched him draw near.

The needle on the talking machine reached the end of the song, then scratched over and over as it continued to revolve, stopping only when the spring had finally wound down. And Ruby, watching the old man in the road, didn't even notice.

At last the man paused in front of her home and gazed around him. Carefully he looked up the road where it crossed the Highland or Mitchell Ditch, and then just as carefully he looked down to where the road dropped off the hill toward American Fork. In both directions the road was empty.

For a long moment then, while Ruby hardly dared to breathe, the man just stood there. But then, with a sudden lifting and resettling of his hat, he reached out, lifted the latch, and walked through Ruby Soderberg Alder's front gate.

Flustered and more than a little frightened, Ruby removed her apron and draped it carefully over the rack next to the damp dish towel. Moving quickly to the mirror, she patted down her hair, noticing as she did so that her fingers were trembling.

"Gray," she muttered to herself, "my hair's so gray. And look how I'm shaking. Law, but I must look old."

Taking a deep breath, Ruby smoothed her dress and was just turning toward the front door so that she could confront the old man, when she heard the sound of an ax striking wood in her backyard. Startled, she hesitated and then moved quickly through the kitchen and washroom and out the back door.

"Here, there, Mister," she called out bravely, "what do you think you're up to?"

Without acknowledging Ruby's presence or her question, the old man continued his swing, striking the wood and splitting it cleanly.

He picked the two pieces up, set them carefully on the small but growing stack, and straightened up, and only then did he turn and face the woman.

"Top of the mornin' to ye, ma'am," he drawled softly, removing his hat as he spoke. "The haythun frost is on the pumpkin, but faith, now, it's almighty purty, just the same."

Startled by the sound of the man's voice, Ruby actually had to force herself to smile and reply.

"It—it *is* beautiful," she stammered.

"Aye, lass, like you. Faith, but ye've been gettin' purtier ev'ry garjus day of yer life, I'm thinkin'."

"Now—now you stop that! You hear?"

"I hear."

"Good. Why—why are you chopping my wood?"

"Man's got to do something to earn his breakfast," the old man replied, his Irish accent gone. "That's one reason."

"Is there another?"

"There surely is, ma'am. I figured the sound of an ax would get you out here so that I—uh, into the sun, I mean."

"I don't understand," Ruby said quickly. "What does the sun have to with anything?"

"Holy Michael O'Murphy, ma'am, ye don't understand because ye haven't looked at yer'self. Shure and I was thinkin' that if I was to meet ye, it would only be fittin' to do so with the sun splashin' over yer beautiful hair. Faith, now, but yer the spittin' image of a Gibson girl."

"Ohhh," Ruby said, fussing with embarrassment, "get along with you and your glib-tongued blarney. I'm an old woman, and you know it."

"I know nothing of the sort. I meant every word I said. Why, if you was to look at yourself now like I am looking at you, it'd likely give you heart palpitations."

"I just *did* look," Ruby declared, patting her hair nervously. "Just before I came out. And I've got to admit, I palpitated alright. Only it surely wasn't because of my ravishing beauty. Besides that, those Gibson girls are all fictitious drawings, and you know it."

"Drawings they are," the old man agreed. "But you are surely the model from which Charles Dana Gibson derives his ideas and his inspiration."

Ruby giggled nervously about the man's foolish compliments. Yet she had the strangest feeling that he meant every silly word he said, and suddenly she was worried. Why would that be? Why would an old man, a vagabond, be speaking to her in such a manner? She didn't know, but just as surely it didn't matter. It couldn't matter.

"Well," she said glibly, deciding to turn the tables on the old man, "you're right. I *am* a Gibson girl, disguised as an old woman. Now, why in heaven's name did you want to meet *me?*"

For an instant the old man was silent, searching for words. Then, with a sudden wink, he grinned and said, "Holy Michael O'Murphy, ma'am. Your fame as a cook has spread far and wide. I just naturally had to see for myself if the legends were true."

Despite herself, Ruby giggled, a strange excitement and embarrassment burning the back of her neck.

"So you're hungry, are you?" she asked.

"Yes, ma'am," he said, suddenly coughing. "It's been most of three days since I've been on the outside of a square meal."

Ruby stared, hardly able to believe he had been so long without food. "Well," she finally declared, "you're not going to pad those ribs of yours standing there. The wash pan's on the bench here on the porch, the towel is clean, and I made the soap only a week past. Just take your time, and I'll see what I can throw together."

"Why, thank you, ma'am. I've been told you're an accommodating lady. But to be truthful, I didn't figure you'd pay me much mind, what with these whiskers and twice-patched overalls I'm wearing. Seems to me, me garjus lass, that there's a great deal more to yer beauty than what first meets the eye."

Acutely aware that she was enjoying the feeling the old man was giving her, Ruby hurriedly spoke: "I never did think whiskers and clothes should make a man."

For an instant the old man gazed steadily at her. "That's uncommon wisdom," he said slowly. "In Proverbs the good Lord declares such a doctrine, but most times us mortals fall shy of the mark when it comes to judging. To my way of thinking, a good woman like you—"

The old man was suddenly seized with another coughing spell, and Ruby was appalled at how weak he looked after it had passed.

"Now see here," she scolded, doing her best to cover her emotions. "You shouldn't talk so much."

The old man grinned. "Folks have always said I was somewhat windy. But about that meal . . ."

"For goodness sake," Ruby said, "listen to me running on. Talk about windy! Other than family, I haven't had a pair of man's boots under my table in nigh onto ten years, and I've most forgotten my manners. Seems to me it's about time I made some changes."

"Well, if there's space under your table and food on top, I'd be happy to help you. And I'll cut wood until it's paid for, too."

"You can cut wood after you've eaten," Ruby stated matter-of-factly. "Man shouldn't go to work on an empty stomach, especially one that's three days empty.

"Uh . . ." Ruby continued, her heart hammering loudly in her chest, "My name is Ruby Alder. And yo—yours?"

For a long moment the old man did not answer. He simply stood, his hands on the ax, gazing into Ruby's eyes. Behind him, in the shed, a chicken squawked in the triumph of a newly-laid egg; and in the corral, Ruby's old milk cow, Jezebel, lowed with the contentment of a new mouthful of cud.

For Ruby, the moment seemed strangely frozen in time, and the tiniest details of life around her became entire worlds of motion. The fly trying to get through the washroom window, Stephen Adam's matched team acting up out in the meadow, the water squirting out of the tap where the early morning ice still blocked the hose, and a dozen other things, all perfectly normal, except that she stood in the middle of them, somehow frozen in that instant of eternity.

"Name, ma'am?" the old man suddenly drawled, breaking the spell. "Faith and I've got me a name. Shure and I'm thinkin' it's been a spell since I used it much, but it's there just the same. Folks who know me call me John."

"And—and your last name, John?" Ruby questioned, doing her best to ignore the roaring that suddenly seemed to fill her ears.

She could see the old man standing there, but he seemed to be a long way off, and he was swaying from side to side, almost as if he were swinging. Yet Ruby knew that it wasn't him who was swinging. It was herself. She felt faint, the roaring in her ears was growing louder.

"Phips," the old man answered, as if from a great distance. "Phips, it is. John William Phips. From England by way of Ireland and the Civil War and a whole lot of lonely wandering since."

Ruby Alder, her temples pounding and her face flushed with emotions that she thought were long dead, gripped the porch post and turned quickly away. How could this be happening to her, she wondered? How was it possible that after all this time she could be feeling this way? Her heart was beating and her face was red as though she were a schoolgirl.

With a valiant effort, she pulled herself together and forced herself to think. He . . . John Phips was standing there waiting. He was hungry. And no matter how she was feeling, no matter how foolish or unreal it all seemed, this man who called himself John needed breakfast. That was where she needed to focus her attention. The rest, if indeed there was any, would surely work itself out in time.

"The—the wash pan is right here, John William Phips," she said, looking him square in the face. "I—I'll be waiting inside, and I'll have your breakfast ready whenever you are ready to eat it."

And with that, Ruby Soderberg Alder turned around and fled into the desperately needed safety of her kitchen.

Chapter 2

John Phips slowly pulled himself away from the table. He had just eaten more of Ruby's bacon and eggs and fried red potatoes than anyone else she had ever fed, and the way he had devoured the peach jam on her homemade biscuits made her think that he had never in his life seen such a thing as preserves.

Slyly she watched from the corner of her eye as he sat back and laced his rheumatic fingers together across his middle. Then he sighed with contentment, eased out one leg so that it would be more comfortable, and looked back at her.

Except for the kettle whistling on the stove and the ticking of the Regulator clock on the wall, the room was silent. And yet with the quiet, there was a strange and unusual peace, and Ruby wondered at it.

Hardly daring to look at her guest, she kept herself busy cleaning up the dishes that had already been washed once that morning. And John Phips did not seem able to keep his eyes off her, of which fact Ruby was painfully aware.

"Ruby, me darlin' lass," he said at last, breaking the long silence, "ye've done yerself proud. Legends are fine, but they don't come near the mark as far as yer fixins' are concerned."

"John Phips," she replied almost sternly, "get along with that blarney."

"No blarney, ma'am. Simple truth. You're a good cook."

"Thank you." Ruby was pleased, and her face showed it. She smoothed her apron with her hands.

"A woman should be a good cook."

Rising, John Phips limped to the back door and surveyed the yard and corrals.

Ruby looked out past him, trying to see her property from his perspective. Her place had been well built, and it showed. But so too did the years when no man had been about to keep things in repair. She had tried, and so had her son, William. But she wasn't up to such work, and her son had grown so busy with his own life that now he hardly had time to stop at all.

John Phips ran his fingers through his hair and returned to the chair by the table. He looked up at her and suddenly grinned.

"I'm a good cook myself," he said. "Had to be."

Startled by such a declaration from a man, Ruby looked at him. But he said no more, and so Ruby began, for the third time, to wipe the cabinet top.

"I—I knew a John Phips once," she said hesitantly. "Long ago."

"I know," the old man answered quietly.

"He's dead!"

For a long moment the old man stared at the table top. Finally he looked up, and his eyes bored into Ruby's.

"Are you sure?" he asked.

"Of course! I . . . the whole town had word, near fifty years ago. He's dead."

"Well, lass," the old man said with a grin, "stranger things have happened. I'm the man you knew, and thanks to your wonderful cooking, I'm not dead yet."

"You don't look like him," Ruby declared emphatically.

John Phips's smile grew wider. "You don't look much like the Ruby Soderberg *I* knew, either. You're prettier now, by far."

Ruby stared at the old man, her mind whirling. Was this the man she had known? But of course he wasn't! That was silly even to consider. That man was hardly even a memory, he was so long dead. And this man, well, he wanted something, and she had better be on her toes.

"What do you intend to do now?" she asked quietly.

Before the old man could reply, a horse came pounding into the yard. A saddle creaked, footsteps sounded on the front porch, and into the room burst a stout, middle-aged man of apparent means.

"Morning, Mother," he almost shouted. "Just passing by, and I wanted to make sure everything was all right.

"Well, hello there, sir," he continued, turning to John Phips. "I didn't know Mother had company."

"I . . . uh . . ." Ruby hesitated. "Willy, uh . . . this is Mr. Phips. John Phips. Mr. Phips, this is my son, William Alder."

Fumbling for his hat, the old man rose to his feet. "It's a pleasure, son. You do favor your mother."

"Uh . . . I suppose so," William responded, doing his best to understand the goings-on in his mother's kitchen. "Did you just come in on the train, sir?"

"Why . . . uh . . . yes, I did. I suppose I look like it too, don't I?"

"Well, I didn't mean it that way," William replied sheepishly. "It's . . . well, it's my job, sort of, keeping track of folks around here."

"What Willy means, Mr. Phips, is that he's the bishop of our ward."

"That's right, sir," William responded. "We're Mormons, of course, and small geographical areas are called wards. I guess I'm what you would call the pastor of our congregation. Fact is, we'll be meeting day after tomorrow morning at ten o'clock sharp. If you're still in town, you'd be welcome to join our worship service."

John and Ruby glanced at each other, and Ruby dropped her eyes.

"I'd be right proud to come," John Phips replied. "If I'm still in town, then count on me being there. I haven't partaken of the emblems of the Lord's Supper in some time, and it would be a pleasure to do so."

"Do you have a place to stay?" William asked.

"Uh . . . yes, he does," Ruby answered. "Yes, he does."

"Well, that's fine. Mother, I must be running along. Seems to be a bit of trouble at the newspaper office, and apparently I'm the only one who can take care of it. I'll chat with you after meeting on Sunday. It's been a pleasure to meet you, Mr. Phips. I hope to see you then, as well."

With a polite nod, Bishop William Alder turned and made his

way out the door. The sound of the departing horse echoed in the room, and for another long moment the clock and the teakettle made the only sounds.

"Willy, huh?" the old man mused. "Seems like a fine man. And a bishop to boot."

Turning, then, he gazed at Ruby, who began fidgeting with her apron.

"Willy is quite famous," she declared. "He writes political editorials, and they are printed in newspapers throughout the nation."

"Willy . . . Willy Alder . . . My goodness, is he *the* Will Alder?"

"One and the same," Ruby declared proudly.

"Does he own the newspaper here in town?"

"Oh, no. The *American Fork Citizen* is owned by William Loveless, from over in Payson. But Willy has his office next door, and as a favor to Loveless, Willy is acting as editor. And of course that means his editorials are first published here."

"You must be very proud."

"I am."

"Well, Ruby Alder, I'm reluctant to change the subject, but just where is it that I'm to spend the night?"

"I . . . uh . . . uh . . ."

"Don't ye worry yer purty little head about it, me wee lass. Ye've a fine barn out back, and if yer cow won't mind the haythun company, I'm thinkin' I'd be delighted to bunk there."

"The—the barn?" Ruby questioned, her voice betraying relief that she didn't understand at all. "Why, I—"

"Good," John Phips replied, grinning. "Then it's all settled. Thank you for that lovely repast, ma'am. I'll be along now. By night, if you'll be good enough to give me a hand at sharpening that ax, you'll have enough wood to last for some time."

"I'd be pleased to help," Ruby said quickly, surprised at the eagerness she felt.

And with that, John Phips arose and escorted Ruby Soderberg out of her door.

Chapter 3

John Phips held the ax lightly in his hands, his thumb expertly feeling the rough edge of the blade. "It's been a spell since this ax had a decent edge."

"I know," Ruby said with a sigh. "I've tried sharpening it, but I just can't do it by myself."

"You shouldn't even try."

"Willy told me he would do it, but he's so busy."

"He looks busy. Tell you what—I'll turn the grindstone if you'll hold the ax."

Ruby smiled. "I'll be glad to. To be honest, that ax has been driving me crazy."

The grindstone was a heavy, old-fashioned type and turned heavily. John Phips started the stone turning, and the rasping whine of steel against stone cut into the clear, still air of the morning. Stopping the grinder, he poured water into the funnel-shaped can that allowed drops to fall slowly on the turning stone.

"How long have you lived in Highland?" he asked as he started the wheel turning once again.

"Most of thirty years," Ruby answered as she worked to hold the blade in place. "My folks came into the Salt Lake Valley from Sweden back in '58 and settled in South Cottonwood. From there we went to Sanpete, and took up land in Moroni. I was living there when I—I married Mr. Alder. We were only there a short time before we came here, and I haven't budged since."

John stood up, stretched, and looked carefully around. "It's a good place," he said quietly. "Good stone house, adequate barn and corrals, even an anvil and forge and tools there in your shed. Do you still keep horses?"

"Not anymore," Ruby answered, smiling. "In fact, that forge hasn't been fired in at least ten years. Mr. Alder always insisted on shoeing his own horses, and from time to time he did a lot of blacksmithing for others."

John started the stone turning again, and quickly the ax showed an edge, carefully honed down.

He straightened, taking the ax from Ruby's hands. "What's that building yonder?"

"It was our granary."

"Mighty big doors for a granary."

Ruby brushed back her hair. "Yes, they are. I had those doors put on this past spring. Now the building is a garage."

"A garage? You mean . . ."

"That's right," Ruby declared proudly. "I own one of the five automobiles in Highland, a brand new 1910 Oldsmobile Special."

A grin spread slowly across the face of John Phips. "A horseless carriage, is it? And can you drive it, Ruby Alder?"

Ruby pulled herself up to her full stature. "Of course I can drive it," she declared. "I have even changed a tire, though a neighbor boy helped me some."

"I meant no disrespect," John said easily. "Knowing you as I think I do, I'd guess you would be a fine driver. In fact, I'm surprised you don't have another granary with a flying machine inside."

A dreamy look came over Ruby's face. "A flying machine," she said. "I've heard they're wonderful inventions. I hope one day I'll be able to see one."

"And fly in one too, no doubt."

"Oh, yes! In fact, I'd like to—"

Ruby, suddenly realizing that she was showing the giddy excitement of a young lady being courted, stopped in confusion.

"I—I'm sorry," she said. "I dream too much, and my son says that I talk too much about my dreams."

"He doesn't approve of dreams?"

"Not for women, I'm afraid. He didn't want me to purchase the Oldsmobile. He says that a woman, especially an *old* woman, has no business doing any sort of business at all. I told him stuff and non-sense, but it didn't change his thinking any.

"He says that when I drive my motor car, I have no dignity. And he hates even more to hear me talk about flying machines. I told him once that I thought they were the transportation of the future and that I wanted to live long enough to ride in one. He was terribly upset with me. Sometimes," and now Ruby giggled, "sometimes I worry that Willy is a bit of a stuffed shirt."

John smiled. "We all have to learn," he said. "I saw a flying machine once, and I think you're right. To see a man actually soaring through the air, not just gliding or ballooning but actually soaring with power and controls, why, it gave me goose bumps."

"You actually saw one *fly?*" Ruby asked breathlessly.

"I did. I was in Dayton, Ohio, last year, and saw both Wilbur and Orville Wright make flights at their Dayton homecoming celebration."

"What . . . was it like?"

"Oh," the old man said enthusiastically as he lifted his arm to explain, "it was one of the grandest sights of my life. Imagine an automobile that has left the road and is climbing up in the air—an automobile without any wheels, we will say, but with white wings instead, like a great huge bird. Well now, imagine this automobile with its wings spread twenty feet each way, coming right toward you with a tremendous flap and roar of its propellers, and you'll have something like what I saw."

Ruby looked dreamily into the distance. "Isn't it marvelous," she said, "to be living in a day when the good Lord has brought such wondrous things to pass?"

"That it is, Ruby, that it is."

For a moment there was a silence; and then, in a quiet voice, John Phips broke it.

"And as for dreaming, Ruby Alder, don't you ever stop. A man, *or a woman,* who can't dream, isn't worth a belch in a high wind."

Ruby giggled. "I declare, you must be a fan of Alice Roosevelt."

"That I am," John answered. "Alice *and* her father. President Roosevelt is a great man, and I love the spirit of his daughter. Furthermore, I've read Shaw, Ibsen, and Zola, and I agree with them and the others who hold that women are the equal of men, or at least ought to be. After the war I met a woman who'd been a spy for the Confederates, and it was said that she had no peers in that terrifying and normally male profession. I also heard that a woman helped the Wright brothers design or build their flying machine. I don't know if that's true, but I do know that Jesus Christ, the greatest exemplar of all, spent a great deal of his earthly ministry in the company of women. He even chastised one of them, Martha by name, for being impatient with another dreamer such as yourself—a woman named Mary.

"Now, Ruby Alder, I've raised a verbal wind again, and I've done it long enough. If you'll excuse me, I'll be about earning my breakfast and a little more besides."

John then went to work, and Ruby climbed her porch steps and entered her home. For the rest of the day, she watched from her window as the old man worked about her yard. She didn't go back outside, yet neither did she go far from her window. Instead, she drew up a chair and sat with her knitting, watching intently as he went about the tasks he had set for himself.

Taking the sharpened ax, he went to the woodpile, which was composed of several logs and two or three old stumps. His first swing split the log he had chosen, and for an hour he worked slowly but steadily, even methodically.

And as she watched, Ruby marveled. Despite his age, John Phips had an easy rhythm in his movements. He didn't work fast, but neither did he waste effort, and shortly he had cut through the largest of the logs. Then he cut through it again and again, and then he split those sections into kindling and firewood.

Ruby continued to marvel, but she was also filled with a sudden aching loneliness, a feeling she hadn't experienced in years. It was John Phips who caused that feeling, she knew that. And yet even with the knowing, she could not stop watching. His movements were so familiar, so ingrained into her thinking that she could hardly deal with her emotions.

Yet it was an old, gray-haired man who stood out there chopping wood, while the image in her mind was of a young man with dark hair and powerful, rippling muscles. But so much seemed the same—the way he rested occasionally on the ax handle, the way he lifted his hat and wiped his brow, the way he smiled when he spoke.

Might this man truly be John Phips? So much seemed to fit, and yet nothing really fit at all. The man she had known was dead, and this old man might just be using his name to . . . to . . . Well, *why* would he be using that name? And how could he seem so much like . . .

Angry with herself, Ruby walked to the water bucket and fetched herself a drink.

What is wrong with you? she asked herself. *Why does this old man cause your heart to pound and your breath to feel like it was caught in your throat? How on earth could you, an old woman of seventy years and one month, be feeling like a giddy schoolgirl?*

For nearly forty years she had been married, and for ten years since the death of her husband she had associated with the good men of her church and community, but almost never had she felt like this.

Moreover, and this was far worse, Ruby was certain that John Phips knew how she felt. Yet he did not look like a man who had had much to do with women. He was friendly enough, yes. But he was also remote, and—the woman in her told her this—he was lonely.

Yet he was a man who shielded his loneliness well. He covered it with his ready smile, his glib tongue, and, perhaps most of all, his wandering. Yet even that made her wonder. Had he never had a home? Had he never had a woman who could penetrate and ease his loneliness?

Or would the likenesses never end?

Finished with the wood, John sank the ax into one of the stumps so that it would not rust, and then while Ruby watched from behind her curtain, he walked into the shed.

Moments later she saw him at the rear of the barn, where recent rains had washed under the foundation timbers, gouging out a dangerous hole. This he filled with gravel from the ditch, tamped hard with the shovel handle. Then he found a large rock, which he rolled to where the runoff fell, positioning it so that the next rainfall would hit the rock and splash away from the barn where it would do no further damage.

Next Ruby watched as he mended the gate to the corral, stoking up the old forge and doing a bit of smithing to repair the hinges. And when that was finished, she stared in open-mouthed amazement as he heated her husband's branding iron and proceeded to rope and brand the rapidly maturing calf that her cow had given birth to the previous spring.

Was there nothing the man could not do? Would he never stop filling her with thoughts and emotions and memories that ought to have been long dead? Why had he come, and what sort of a spell was he weaving that she had so little ability—

"Ma'am?"

Spinning, Ruby was startled to see John standing in the doorway. "Y-yes?"

"Didn't mean to startle you, but the sun's about to set, and I was wondering if I might have permission to quit for the day so's I could go into town and pick me up a shirt."

"Permission?" she asked blankly.

"Yes'm. I reckon as long as you're feeding and boarding me, I ought to clear my goings and comings with you."

"John Phips," she stormed, suddenly angry, "I am *not* your master!"

"No ma'am," he answered, grinning, "you aren't. But you are my employer, and I never worked for one more lovely. And your eyes flash when you get excited. Did you know that?"

Ruby, stretched beyond what any one woman could possibly endure in a single day, looked at the wrinkled, grinning face of the man who had caused her consternation, and then she did the only sensible thing she could have done. She clutched her hands at her sides, her arms stiff, her face rigid, and fervently uttered a single solitary order.

"Go!" she said as her eyes grew large and her brows furrowed. "Gooo!"

And John Phips, with a youthful smile still playing on his tired old face, went.

Day 2

Saturday
October 22, 1910

Chapter 4

"Ruby," John Phips said with a sigh as he pulled back from the table, "I have never in my life tasted finer pork chops."

Ruby blushed, thinking that it had been ten years since she had received such a compliment. "You're just saying that, John Phips." she said.

"Aye, lass. Of course I'm sayin' it. That doesn't make it any less true. Faith, and I'll tell you something else, me darlin'. That peach cobbler tasted like it was made in heaven and carried here by angels, just for me."

"Stuff and nonsense," Ruby argued, smiling coyly. "You probably talk like that with all the ladies."

"Nope," John replied, "I don't. Truth is, Ruby, there aren't any other lady friends. Never have been."

John Phips had been busy that day. Steadily, since breakfast, he had been painting, putting a white coat on the dilapidated picket fence around Ruby's home. And again, as she had throughout the entire day before, Ruby had watched, fascinated.

He had not worked fast, but he worked steadily, and she had been amazed at his progress. The painting of the fence was now complete, and he had some planking in place on some old sawbucks so that he could start on the trim of her home. He was remarkable, and she knew that if she fed him every meal for a month, she could not pay him for all he had accomplished.

Apparently he had learned much in his life, and he seemed able to do anything he set his hand to do. But to think that he had spent his life alone . . .

"Oh, John," she declared, "I don't mind if you speak of other women."

"I would speak of 'em if there'd been any. But there haven't. All my life, I've just been waiting for you."

For a moment Ruby looked into John's blue-gray eyes. And then, to hide the tears that were filling her own eyes, she arose and began clearing the dishes.

"My turn to wash," John abruptly declared, getting up and grabbing the apron from its nail.

"Now, you sit down, John Phips. This is woman's work, and after painting all that fence, you need to rest."

"Fiddlesticks," John said as he began ladling hot water into the pan. "You're the one who has worked hard today. I've just spent a few hours on the dumb end of a paintbrush, is all. Now, hand me those dishes and grab a towel. We'll have this job done in no time, and then I can hike down into American Fork before all the stores close."

"But you just went yesterday."

"I did. But it took me so long to get there that the stores were closed. I still need that new shirt."

"Well," Ruby declared, smiling, "I can take care of that. You crank up the Oldsmobile, and I'll have you down in town in a jiffy."

"Now, Ruby, you don't need to do that."

"John, for two days you have worked like a slave for me. Giving you a ride is the least I can do."

For a moment he said nothing, but at last he grinned. "Shure and ye've got yerself a deal, me garjus lass. Now hand me those dishes."

For a few minutes they worked in silence, and Ruby watched the man with the familiar name, looking for characteristics that might help her to know. He limped, and that was not the same. His hands were gnarled and a little twisted, but that would be age, as would the wrinkles in his face and his white hair. Those things she couldn't consider.

His eyes, as far as she could remember, were the same. He also had some very disturbing mannerisms, little traits that reminded her of the man she had known, briefly, so many years before. Then there was his Irish brogue and blarney. Those too had been traits of a very young John Phips.

There were other questions, many of them. Yet how could she possibly ask them all? She would seem so forward. She just could not bring herself to pry.

So was it him? She honestly didn't know. But deep inside, a strange little voice seemed to be telling her yes. And more and more, Ruby Alder was starting to believe that voice.

Thirty minutes after the dishes were done, Ruby pulled the long black Oldsmobile touring car to an abrupt and dusty stop outside the Jackson Gents' and Boys' Clothing Store on Main Street in American Fork. As Ruby pushed back the magneto, the car shuddered to a stop, and nimbly she climbed out.

"Come on," she said to the ashen-faced John Phips. "Let's go in and—John, is anything wrong?"

John opened his eyes. "I—I don't think so. Am I still alive?"

"Alive? Of course you're alive. What are you talking about?"

"I don't—I—Ruby, who on earth taught you to drive?"

"Nobody. I just figured it out by myself."

John sighed. "I thought so."

"Why do you ask?"

"Uh . . . Ruby, why don't *I* drive us home?"

"But John—"

"Ruby, it's only good manners. A gentleman *always* drives, and the lady sits and enjoys the tour."

"Really?" Ruby asked incredulously.

"Absolutely. And while I'm driving, watch me closely. I'm certain you can pick up a few pointers—things such as proper speed, how to stay on the road, how to slow for flocks of chickens and herds of cattle and gaggles of geese and folks' careless children. You know, the sorts of things that might damage your car should you run over them."

Ruby smiled. "John, of course you can drive. And I will watch. Willy won't teach me how to be a motorist, won't even get in the motorcar with me, and so I've been desperate for someone to teach me. Besides, Marshall Hamilton told me just the other week that I drove far too fast for the public good. I just don't know how to drive more slowly."

"I'll show you," John said.

"Good. And John, I'm so glad that you aren't one of those awful men who say terrible things about women drivers."

"Terrible things?" John asked, feeling suddenly uncomfortable.

"Yes, jokes and tales. Just last Sunday my grandaughter Allyson told me one. It goes, 'Papa, how can you tell that Mommy is a woman driver?' Answer: 'Because she's always running somebody down.'"

John did his best not to snicker. "That—that's not very funny, is it," he stated quickly.

"Not very. If they would just make rules instead of those cruel jokes and stories, I would live by them."

"Oh, they're trying, Ruby. Here and there, folks are trying to put a few rules in place. In Vermont it's illegal to drive an automobile unless somebody runs along out in front waving a red flag. That tends to slow folks down, though it might be rough on the flag-carrier, happen the driver gets careless. In Tennessee it's illegal to drive anywhere unless the motorist has posted a notice at least a week in advance, outlining his trip. A law such as that would surely promote planning ahead."

"How awful!" Ruby declared. "The next thing you know they'll be telling me I can only drive on one side of the road."

"Might at that," John agreed.

"Well," Ruby said as she untied her hat and unbuttoned her colorful duster that had only recently come by mail order from Saks and Company of New York City, "let's go in and get your shopping done. Joseph and William Jackson are good friends of mine. They'll fit you up with a suit in no time."

"Suit? Ruby, I came for a shirt. A shirt is all I can afford."

"I know that, John. But I owe you much more than a suit would cost. Besides, you need one."

"Why do I need a suit?"

"Well, for church tomorrow, silly. Besides, Monday they're laying the cornerstone for our new tabernacle here in American Fork, and I have been invited as one of the guests of honor. You will be escorting me, and so obviously you need a suit."

"Ruby, I don't know. I try not to get in public too often."

"John, don't be silly. Now take my arm and let's hurry. I also need to visit Manda and Ida Chipman's Millinery, and I am completely out of corn plasters and St. Jacob's Oil. Thomas Steele has been holding them for me in his drugstore all week, and we simply *must* pick them up."

"Does he sell sodas?"

"He does."

"Then let's be going, my sweet. I'm in the mood for a red raspberry soda. And I'll buy, if they aren't over a dime."

Ruby laughed, and together they entered the Jackson Gents' and Boys' Clothing Store. Neither of them saw the man who stood across the rutted street, gazing steadily off in the other direction.

Chapter 5

"Hello, Mother."

"Well, hello, Willy. This is a surprise."

Willy looked about his mother's neat home. "I was out here on the bench, so I thought I'd drop by. Can we talk?"

"Of course. Sit down there in Mr. Alder's horsehair rocker and tell me what is on your mind."

"Mother, when I say talk, I mean alone."

"All right."

"I mean, is that old man—"

"Mr. Phips."

"Yes, Mr. Phips. Might he walk in on us?"

"Oh, I doubt it. He's out getting an early start on digging the potatoes, and I imagine he'll be busy until dark."

"He does seem busy."

"Yes, Willy, he's marvelous! Have you seen all that he's done? And in only two days. I'm so thrilled."

"Yes," Willy replied, scowling, "he has kept himself occupied. Pretty nigh becoming indispensable, isn't he?"

"Well, I wouldn't go *that* far," Ruby answered slowly. "Still, I am so thankful for his help."

"Effie McPheeters told me that you bought him a suit and practically an entire wardrobe this afternoon."

"Effie told you *that?*" Ruby asked in surprise. "Well, that old busybody! I always said those telephone operators were nothing but gossips and busybodies. Do you know that every time I use that telephone I have to *ask* her to get off the line? Well, I do, and I think it's a disgrace! Why, I'm of a mind to—"

"Mother, it wasn't Effie's fault that she put through the call from Joe Jackson to his wife. It's her job, you know."

"It isn't her job to listen in!"

"She isn't the only one who's talking, Mother."

"Oh, pshaw, Willy. I'm seventy years old. What on earth are people going to say?"

"Plenty, Mother. In fact, two different women have already asked me what is going on out here."

"Have they really?" Ruby beamed. "Glory be, maybe we'll have a scandal. I haven't ever had a decent scandal, and I've often thought how much fun it would be, having folks all over town just wagging their tongues with juicy nonsense about me. My goodness, I would imagine—"

"Mother, for goodness sake, listen to yourself."

Ruby smiled. "You're right," she declared. "I am being silly, aren't I."

"I'd say so. Now I want to know if it is true. Did you buy that old man some clothing?"

Ruby glared at her son. "I did," she answered defiantly.

"May I ask why?"

"Do you need to ask? Look around you, Willy. That old man, as you insist on calling him, has worked his heart out for two solid days, and he shows no signs of stopping yet. I had to pay him some way, didn't I?"

"Mother, I told you that I was going to do those things."

"Yes, three years ago."

William Alder dropped his head and sighed. Then he looked back at the almost angry woman. "Mother, it isn't my fault my editorials became so popular, or that they called me to be bishop."

"Nor was it mine, Willy. And I wouldn't want it any other way. I'm thrilled to death with your success, and especially with your calling. But I must go on living, and things need to be kept up. Since you're so busy, John has been doing that for me. Now tell me, why are you so worried?"

William sighed. "Mother, I'm concerned for you. I've only been bishop for three months, and twice in that time I've had to deal with situations where vagabonds have taken advantage of innocent

Church members. Sister Lippencroft lost her entire life savings not thirty days ago to that fellow who was going to reroof her home."

"And you think John might be after my money?"

"I'd say the possibility is certainly there. Wouldn't you?"

"I would. I've even thought about it."

"Good," William said. "Then you'll send him on his way."

"No—no, Willy, I won't. At least not yet. John Phips hasn't asked for any money, and I've promised to feed him until he gets my place in order. That should be sometime by the middle of next week. Meanwhile, to be warned is to be prepared. I promise I'll be careful with him."

The bishop sat silently, rocking back and forth. His mother was an intelligent woman, and he knew it. Yet he felt a strange sense of worry, and he didn't know how to get at it. Idly he picked up his mother's new stereoscope and glanced at the double-imaged slide, an image of New York's growing skyline.

"Mother," he said quietly as he put the stereoscope back beside her talking machine and stack of record cylinders, "is there something going on that you aren't telling me?"

"Not telling you?"

"Yes, Mother. Not telling me. Do you know something about that old man that I don't know?"

"I—I—well, why do you ask?"

"Because you aren't acting like yourself."

"Is—is that all?"

"No, it isn't. Since yesterday I have learned some very strange things, and I *think* you are being set up to become my next 'Sister Lippencroft.' Let me tell you a little about that old man out there. He came into town on the 9:15 yesterday morning, asked directions from Luke Savage and Lowell Nelson at the depot, and then proceeded directly to the Highland Road. Ed Tucker gave him a ride in his wagon, and from where Ed let him off, he proceeded directly here. And on his way, he didn't stop off at one other place. Mother, that man was not looking for a good meal. He was looking for *you!*"

Ruby stood and walked nervously to her counter to rearrange the location of her new-fangled bread toaster, wondering what she should say. She knew that she could give Willy a little information, but nothing that was definite. And she wanted to do that, for she would have liked his help.

But on the other hand, she knew Willy Alder very well, and that knowledge made her want to protect the man called John Phips. Willy had a penchant for digging out facts no matter what the cost, for in certain things he was almost unbendable in his personality. Because of that, she was not at all ready to throw that dear old man, *whoever* he really was, to the wolf who wrote those nationally syndicated editorials.

"Willy," she finally said, laughing her son's charges off, "how you do carry on."

"Mother, I fear that old man is up to no good. I can see it in his eyes. He isn't telling you the truth."

"Very few do," she said quietly.

"That's correct, but it doesn't make it right. Would you mind if I talked to Mr. Phips?"

Ruby spun about in surprise. "Do you really want to?" she asked.

"Of course! You know me, Mother. I don't beat about very many bushes. I'll talk to him straight out, and if his answers are satisfactory, then I'll quit worrying. He can stay in town as long as he wants, and with my blessing."

"Very well," Ruby said as she walked to the door. "I'll call him in."

Moments later John Phips stood, battered hat in hand, in Ruby Alder's kitchen. "You wanted to see me?" he asked of the seated William Alder.

"I did. Have a seat."

"Thank you."

John pulled a chair out from the table and sat, while Ruby, sensing the old man's nervousness, remained standing by the counter.

"Frankly, Mr. Phips," William said quietly, "you worry me."

"How's that?"

"Because I've learned a few things about you, and those things give me concern. Why are you here? Or, why are you at my mother's home? Would you mind responding to those questions, Mr. Phips?"

Ruby watched as John sat silently, gazing at her son. Then, without answering, he turned his head and looked steadily at her, momentarily holding her gaze. She dropped her eyes.

John was asking her a question, she knew. But she did not know how to respond. How could she, when . . . when . . .

"Well?"

"What . . . what has your mother told you?"

"Frankly, she has told me very little, and you know that. You've told her practically nothing about yourself, so how could she?"

"Yes," John answered quietly, "I see that you are right."

"So, why are you here?"

"I . . . I was just sort of passing through. I had heard from Ruby's brother about her cooking, and I was hungry. So I thought, well, why not give it a try? I did, she was truly hospitable, and I've just been trying to help her out a little in return."

"That's it?"

"Yes," John answered slowly as he looked at Ruby, "I suppose that's it."

"You're a tramp, then? A vagabond?"

John smiled. "If you mean by that, a wanderer, then the answer is yes."

"Are you employed?"

"Most folks won't talk work with a man as old as I am."

William looked quickly at him. "Yes, I can see that, and I hadn't thought of it. But you do admit that you are broke?"

"No harm in admitting the truth, I suppose. I do have a couple of dollars, so technically—"

"Mr. Phips, if you plan on trying to get my mother's money, then you had better cancel such plans immediately."

"Bishop, I resent that deeply. I respect your mother more than you could ever imagine. When we part, our accounts with each other will be square."

"Willy," Ruby added, "I have told you that John has not done anything to take advantage—"

"Mother," William interrupted, "let me finish."

Turning back to John, he spoke again. "You spoke about when you leave. Will that be soon?"

John's eyes dropped. "I—I'm not certain. I need to . . . to . . . There are many factors . . ."

William sat back in triumph. "Come, Mr. Phips, be honest. Tell us exactly why you are here!"

Miserably John looked from Ruby to her son and back again. "I can't," he answered finally, his voice almost a whisper.

"Can't? Or *won't.*"

"Doesn't much matter, does it?"

"Not at all," William responded. "Mother, I think that you've heard enough."

Ruby stood silently, her face reflecting her pain.

"Reckon I'll finish what I can of the potatoes," John declared as he rose slowly to his feet. "Then I'll be on my way."

Limping slowly, John crossed to the door, opened it, and stepped outside. There was silence then in the home, and finally William stirred uneasily.

"It's for the best, Mother. It truly is."

"All right, Willy," Ruby replied with great resignation. "Whatever you say. I just wish . . ."

"You wish what?"

"I just wish you could get to know him, Willy. I really do."

"Well, under different circumstances—"

"Willy, I can tell you about him, if you'd like. Please let me. I know a great deal, and I am certain you would want—"

But William Alder was looking at the watch he carried in his vest pocket, his mind already elsewhere. "Sorry, Mother, not today. I'm just relieved that he will be going, and you should feel the same way."

Ruby did her best to smile. "Thank you for coming, Willy. That was very sweet of you."

William Alder kissed his mother, and then, after taking a deep breath that indicated his own sense of satisfaction, he strode out the front door, mounted his horse, and was gone.

Ruby watched him for a moment, and then with a sigh she turned and walked to the talking machine. Carefully she wound it up, chose a cylinder from the rack, and put it in place. Then she eased back the spring-drive, setting the record to revolving. Lastly she lifted the needle and set it in the first groove, and while the scratchy strains of "In My Merry Oldsmobile" wafted through the room, she closed her eyes and tried to keep the tears from flowing.

Ruby Alder was worried but trying not to show it. But the worry was there, nevertheless.

Chapter 6

"Nine dollars? Ruby, that is shameful."

"John, stop worrying about it. If we hadn't been in such a hurry, I'd have ordered a tailor-made suit and paid ten dollars. Already you've earned much more than that."

"But Ruby, look at all this. Shoes, suspenders, a linen collar, two shirts, a pair of trousers, and woolen hose. And then on top of that, the suit. Why, you must have spent twenty or twenty-five dollars! I can't let you—"

"John, you've earned it."

"Twenty-five dollars in less than two days? Ruby, that's nonsense, and you know it."

"Well, if you finish digging my potatoes Monday after the meeting, then you surely will have earned it. Now stop fussing and finish that pie and ice cream."

John sighed and took another bite. "I can't do it, Ruby. I'll be leaving in a bit, and there won't be any more of *anything.*"

"John, you don't need to leave."

"According to William, I do. He seemed pretty emphatic about it, too."

"He was. But after all, John Phips, this is *my* home."

"Ruby, did you tell him that we had—had known each other before?"

Slowly Ruby shook her head.

"Why didn't you?"

"I . . . I . . . John, I can't. I don't even know for certain."

"I thought that was it."

"Well, can you blame me? For fifty years a man is dead, and then a stranger walks up and announces that he is the dead man. Would *you* believe that? I need more time, I need—"

"This is wonderful pie, Ruby, me lass."

"Huckleberries. And stop changing the subject. I will not allow you to leave until . . . until . . ."

"And this ice cream is absolutely delicious. Better than any I ever found in Los Angeles when I was staying at the pigeon ranch."

"Joseph Elsmore makes—you *really* spent some time in Los Angeles?"

John quickly looked up. "Did I say that?"

"You did. And you told Willy that my brother had told you about my cooking. Do you really know Jons Soderberg?"

"I do," John replied quietly, "though that isn't his name there. James Y. Johnson, he calls himself. He's mighty proud of you, Ruby. Like I said, it was upon his recommendation that I came here."

"Yes, you did," Ruby stated flatly, not wanting to think the things her mind was telling her. "How is he?"

"Doing well. James's ranch has over a hundred thousand pigeons, I reckon, and the railroad has even built a spur to it for shipping and cash-paying tourists. He does appear to be prosperous."

"And?"

"And what?"

"How is *he?*"

"Ruby, I don't think—"

"John, I want to know!"

"Well," John said with resignation, "he still talks about being bishop and about his horse race from Fountain Green to Salt Lake. He even has that big old Belgian plug down there. Ingersol, I think its name is. The horse is mighty old now, but I doubt it will ever become glue. James thinks too much of it."

"Go on."

"Ruby," John replied with exasperation, "what do you want me to tell you?"

"About his family, John. Anything and everything. Are any of them there?"

"None of his wives. He's still in hiding, and none of them would go with him. I think that stint in prison about did him in. Then, when none of those women would hide with him after he got out on bail, well, he just up and left them behind. Probably wasn't smart, but he did it, and now it's too late to go back and do it all over again the right way.

"But his son Ernest has been with him some, and Johnny and Hyrum, too. Tell the truth, though, I think he's lonely."

"Oh, poor Jons."

"Yeah," John replied quietly, "loneliness is a hard thing, a hard and never-ending thing. At least it seems so. I used to wonder if I would ever . . ."

And then, with a shake of his head, John Phips turned to his companion and smiled.

"Do you have any further questions?"

Ruby stared, her heart pounding. "One," she said, her voice almost a whisper. "Would you roll up your sleeve and show me your left arm?"

John Phips stared silently. Painfully he stood and walked to the doorway, where he turned back and looked at Ruby. Slowly then, and with great care, he unbuttoned the cuff of his shirt. And then he began to roll it up.

Chapter 7

"Faith now, Ruby me lass, but why don't we take in the ayv'nin sunset together out on yer front porch swing."

Bashfully, Ruby giggled. Then the two of them cleared off the table and banked what was left of the ice cream inside the wooden icebox.

Later, as they sat together on the screen porch, John Phips spoke. "You do have a fine home here."

"I've enjoyed it."

"Mr. Alder must have been a good husband for you."

"He was, John. And though I was his polygamous wife, he did his best to take care of me and treat me with the same respect he showed his first wife. She and I were good friends, too, and she was a dear, dear woman. I think we got along so well because he was the sort of man he was."

"Well, the place shows that he was a good man."

Curiously Ruby looked at him. "How can you tell that? From my home, I mean."

"Oh, I can see more in a place than you might think. Over the years I've kicked around quite a bit, and a man learns. For instance, there has been a great deal of work done here, good solid work that a man ought to be proud of. That tells me that your husband took pride in what he built."

"He did, but tell me what you see that can tell you that."

John smiled and leaned back in the swing. "First is your home. If he built it, he knew his business. If he hired it done, then the craftsman did. The stone has been well cut and fitted carefully, and the house sits on the highest point of land on your place. Forty or fifty years ago, it would have been easy to defend your home from marauding Indians. One good man with a rifle and enough food and water could hold it indefinitely."

"They had Indian troubles here for a time," Ruby declared. "Both the Walker and Blackhawk wars affected this area. Most folks could fort up in a hurry, and up in Alpine the Moyle family even built a stone tower to defend themselves. I don't recall hearing if it was ever used, but it was there—in fact, it still is."

John nodded. "I've seen a little Indian trouble myself from time to time."

Silence followed, not strained, but easy, and in it they both drifted off into memories, recalling a life now mostly past.

"What else do you like about the place?" Ruby asked, wanting to hear more of John Phips's voice.

"What else? Well, the corrals have been well built. They need work, but they're strong and should last for years to come. So should the shed, though its roof needs to be reshingled. Your garden was once a fine and well-watered piece of land, but the dams are mostly gone, and the ditches are grown in with weeds. Your well is deep, and the water is clear and cold, but I've never in my life heard such a squeaky pump. If you have any grease, I'll take care of that first thing Monday morning. So it's a fine place. It just needs the hand of a man who can make do."

Ruby didn't answer that, for she had no idea what to say. On one hand, John might have been saying that Willy ought to do more to help her out. One part of her thought so too, but the other part, the mother part, looked upon her son with patient tenderness and hoped that he wouldn't always be so busy.

On the other hand, John might have been making an offer, an offer of himself. But did she want that? It was an intriguing thought, but also unsettling. It had been forever since she had had a full-time man about, and she had grown quite used to her independence. Besides that, there were a lot of unanswered questions about the man who sat next to her on the swing, even if he was the man she used to know.

Still, John Phips had crept into her thoughts in a way that frightened her but also left her breathless with hope, and so she didn't know, she didn't know . . .

"Your boy, William, is quite a man."

Startled, Ruby felt the strangest let-down. John *was* talking about her son. The offering of himself was simply the foolish dream of an old lonely woman, a woman who ought to learn once and for all to obey her son and stop dreaming.

"He's never given me a bit of trouble," she declared almost defensively. "In fact, he's spent his whole life trying to make mine easier. Don't know what I would have done without him, especially these past ten years. To my motherly way of thinking, he's a mighty honorable and handsome man."

"Well, like I said, he does favor you, Ruby."

"In looks, maybe. I haven't ever been as good a person as he is. He's terribly busy, but good. Smart, too. I think he must have picked those traits up from his father."

"Now, don't think too harshly of yourself, Ruby. We're all different folks, and that's the way the good Lord made us to be. You raised him, and you did a fine job of it. That's why you can tell me honestly that he's such a good man."

"Yes, I suppose you're right. I just don't know what to do about him and you. I would never have thought that he . . . that he . . ." Ruby's voice drifted off, and for a moment there was silence.

"Well," John declared finally, "I could tell he was some displeased with me. He surely does want me to go."

"Oh, he'll come around, John."

"Perhaps. Are you going to tell him that you knew me once?"

"I—I—don't think I'd dare. Willy is an investigator of the first order, and I'm not at all certain that I want to know what he might find."

"That's a very honest answer, Ruby."

"Yes, I believe in honesty. Do you?"

John stared off into the evening. "I do," he said slowly. "Sometimes, though, a man gets himself into a position . . . But enough on that. I am John Phips, the man you knew so long ago. And I would like to find a way to tell William that bit of news."

"It will happen, John. All in good time, though."

"Well, the good bishop is getting a bit impatient."

Ruby tried to smile. "He's just not used to seeing me with a man, John. After all, Henry Alder has been dead almost ten years, and I'm just past seventy, myself."

"Holy Michael O'Murphy," John exclaimed, "I'd 'ave bet good money that you weren't a day over fifty-two."

"Johnny." Ruby giggled and felt very surprised that she had dared use such an informal name. "You're awful, do you know that?"

The man grinned, "I reckon I am. But you like it, don't you."

Ruby glowed anew and then closed her eyes, in heaven with her thoughts. It really was him. Goodness but that was something! She almost giggled, just thinking of it. It was all crazy, totally insane, but still there were her feelings and the mark on his arm, and now the old man had proved it beyond doubt. Besides, there was the warm and wonderful way that he made her feel . . .

The two aging people rocked in silence then, each warmed with the memories of the past two days, and neither wanting to say anything that would break the spell of what was taking place.

At last, piecing together a lot more courage than he knew he had, John reached up and scratched his neck. Then gradually he worked his hand back to his trousers, inched it closer to Ruby's hand, and then hesitantly pulled it back.

Ruby, suddenly aware of her companion's intentions, and aware too of the man's obvious inexperience, gently reached out and placed her hand over his trembling fingers.

For a moment John Phips's entire frame stiffened with fear. But then, as Ruby felt his muscles relax, she laid her head gently against his shoulder.

Off in the west, the sun slipped quietly down behind the mountains. Behind them, where the American Fork Canyon sliced through the northern reaches of Mount Timpanogos, the gold of the sunset climbed rapidly upward until only the highest peaks remained aglow. Then these peaks, too, grew dark; and in the deepening twilight John Phips carefully, fearfully, placed his arm around the shawl-covered shoulders of Ruby Alder.

"I'm glad you came here yesterday," the elderly woman said quietly, breaking the long silence.

"Reckon I am, too," John replied huskily.

The twilight deepened, and the silence grew with it. Ruby kept her eyes on the last of the lighted sky, and John Phips, watching her, wondered that anyone could be so beautiful.

"Are you a happy woman, Ruby?" he asked, almost in a whisper.

"Yes I am."

"And have you always been?"

"Oh, I've known sadness," Ruby countered thoughtfully. "But William and my husband have eased that with their goodness."

"I'm glad," John replied. "You deserve happiness."

Slowly, John Phips paused and took a deep breath. "Besides your son, William, do you have any other children?"

"Well, Botilda, Henry Alder's first wife, had thirteen, nine of whom are still living. I always felt that I was their mother, just as Botilda was."

"What—what about you?"

"No, Willy was my only child. And you, John?"

John Phips coughed. "Like I told you, Ruby—there's never been anyone in my life . . . until you."

"Oh, Johnny, you must have been so lonely."

"Well, I have been, from time to time. Still, a man gets along as best he can. A long time ago, almost in a different lifetime, I had a memory that caused a powerful load of loneliness. Strangely, that same memory, of you, has also kept me happy—until I found you yesterday."

"Willy thinks you're after my money," Ruby said with a girlish giggle.

"That's what he said. And maybe I am. Do you have much?"

"Oh, I have sufficient for my needs . . . and then just a little bit more. Henry took good care of me."

"Then you'd better be careful," John said with a grin. "If you judge me by the outfit I'm wearing, your son has every reason to worry."

Again there was silence—long and deep, but increasingly comfortable.

"What . . . what have you done in your life?" Ruby finally

asked. "I feel like I have known you forever, and yet I don't know anything about you."

"Well," John said with a sigh, "actually, there's nothing much to tell."

"Oh, there must be something, Johnny. I think that you're just being modest."

"No," he replied, "not really. There was my mission to the Eastern States. And then one night a band of Confederates raided a town where I was staying, and they hit the house where I was being boarded. I was wounded, and the next thing I knew I was in that Confederate prison camp. The bullet wound, here where the scar is on my head, made me forget things, and for a long time I even forgot who I was. But I already told you that."

"Well, after the war then, Johnny. What came next?"

"Oh, nothing—at least nothing much to tell about. I still couldn't remember much about myself, and I couldn't find anyone else who knew anything either. I thought I must have been a soldier, but I never could find any records with the war department. So for quite a spell I did odd jobs and just lived from day to day. Did some whaling, too—went around the Horn a couple of times. Matter of fact, I went clear to China once. That was a fine voyage, and the captain wasn't a bad man, either. Mostly though, I reckon I've just been drifting along, earning a dollar or two here and there, just waiting."

"Waiting?" the elderly woman asked, almost timidly.

"Yes," John whispered, quietly and peacefully. "Waiting to . . . to find myself. Once I did that, then I began waiting to find just the right woman."

"Oh, Johnny," Ruby replied, her voice quivering with emotion. "Have you . . . have you found her?"

Smiling into the increasing darkness, John Phips did not reply. Instead, he quietly and securely took Ruby's other shoulder, pulling her around to face him.

Then, in the quiet of the night, as the man and woman looked into each other's eyes, John leaned forward and kissed Ruby tenderly on the forehead. Then he held her tightly against him.

"I . . ." Ruby paused as she pulled away, searching for breath and for words all at once. "I . . . I think I love you, Johnny Phips."

"I surely do hope so, ma'am," he muttered, his voice low. "I reckon I love you, too. Fact is, I've loved you in my mind ever since I can remember. I just wish I could have found you sooner."

"I do too, Johnny. But I guess it just wasn't to be."

"No, I suppose not. But I'll tell you what, Ruby Alder. We'll have us a grand old time now that I *have* found you!"

Ruby giggled, and the two were snuggling together again in the cool of the October evening when a pot shattered at the side of the porch. That was followed by a gasp of fear, and then silence.

"Goodness!" Ruby exclaimed as she sat up.

"Sounded like a flower pot," John declared as he pulled himself to his feet. "I wonder—"

Ruby, also standing, suddenly put her finger over John's mouth. "Listen," she whispered.

Together the couple stood, and out in the darkness of Ruby's yard there was a whispered question and answering giggle. That was followed by running footsteps, and again John and Ruby were alone.

"Who was that?" John asked.

"It doesn't matter," Ruby answered quietly as she took John's arm in her hands. "Now, are we going to stand here all night, or do you have a little snuggled-up swinging left in you?"

In the darkness John smiled, and together the two sat back down to enjoy each other and the chilly October night.

Day 3

Sunday
October 23, 1910

Chapter 8

"Top o' the mornin', me beautiful lass."

Ruby, excited but instantly flustered, stood at the back door of her home, gazing upon the freshly shaved and Sunday-dressed John Phips. Without knowing that she did so, she nervously patted her hair and smoothed her dress.

"I . . . uh . . . Johnny, you look so very nice."

"Thank you," he answered simply. "So do you."

"That suit is very becoming on you."

John grinned. "Feels good, too. It's been quite a spell since I had Sunday-go-to-meeting clothes like these. Are you ready?"

"Let me get my shawl," Ruby smiled, "and I will be."

A little later, John pulled the Oldsmobile to a stop outside the meetinghouse in American Fork where Ruby's ward met. A few horses shied as the car clattered up beside them, but the sight and sound of automobiles was becoming common enough that most horses, and their drivers, were used to the commotion and did not go into full fright.

"My lady," John said gallantly as he helped Ruby to the ground, "may I escort you to your pew?"

"You certainly may, good sir," she replied with a flourish. And together the two entered the church and walked to their seats.

For a moment they sat in silence, listening to the organist's rendition of a hymn designed to keep the congregation in a reverant mood. John sat without moving, but his eyes were busy scanning every inch of the chapel, missing nothing, cataloging in his mind the whereabouts of the people, the doors, and so on.

"It truly has been a spell," he finally whispered.

"Since you went to church?" Ruby questioned in surprise.

"Yes. Especially in a regular church building. There was a branch in Los Angeles, but it was so far across town that I only got there once. I went with your brother James. Back in Ohio and down in Texas there were hardly any members at all, and only occasionally could I find a branch to meet with. This feels good, mighty good."

"What is he like, Johnny?"

"Your brother?"

"Uh-huh. Tell me about his spirit."

"Well, like I told you, I think it was about broken when his family wouldn't go to Los Angeles with him. He still doesn't understand that. And that's why he's never been back up to visit. What's more, I don't think he'll ever come back."

"Does he . . . is he still active in the Church?"

"Of course he is. He believes it with all his heart and supports it every way he can. The missionaries live with him at no cost to them, and he regularly holds meetings on the ranch for them and their investigators. In fact, one day he and I were standing on the corner when two missionaries called together a street meeting. They got it going and the one elder was just getting into his sermon when a few ruffians started to harrass him.

"James didn't take kindly to that, so he stepped to the front and invited any of those fellows to start their anti-socializing off with him.

"Now James is still big and powerful, and I've never known anyone who could beat him for sheer brute strength. A couple of those boys set at him, not really seeing clearly who it was they were dealing with. But it didn't take long for your brother to set the record straight."

"What did he do?"

"Oh, not much. He took hold of their necks with those stove-plate hands of his, lifted them into the air, and cracked their thick and unrepentant skulls together. Made quite an impression on them, too. They slept for a while after that, real peaceful-like; the others were quiet as could be, and each of the elders got off a real fine sermon. All in all, James was a terrific support to the Church that day. And active too, if you know what I mean."

Ruby smiled. "Jons is such a good man."

"Well, good morning, Mother."

Startled, Ruby looked up into the smiling face of her son.

"Good morning, Willy," she beamed. "Beautiful day, isn't it."

"It is at that. Unusual for this time of year. So you're still here, Mr. Phips."

"I am."

"Well, we welcome you to our meeting. I . . . uh . . .well, I might as well say it now as later. I learned in bishopric meeting this morning that a fellow was asking about you yesterday. Said he was from Los Angeles."

"Oh?" John asked casually. "Did he have a name?"

"I didn't hear it. Heard he was a small man, though, fiftyish or sixtyish. Looked official, too. Oh, and one other thing—he carried a detective's badge." William Alder smiled. "I thought you might want to know."

"Thank you," John Phips replied, nodding politely. "God bless you with your meeting."

William Alder stood still for an instant, uncertain. It looked to Ruby as if he had expected John to bolt, or at least to make some response other than what he had. When nothing else happened, however, he walked to the stand, and John and Ruby sat silently together.

"Johnny," Ruby finally whispered, "do you know what Willy is talking about?"

"Hard to say," John replied easily. "Fellows come and fellows go, they tell tales, and sometimes the truth isn't in them at all. I'd have to see the man myself to be certain. Might even be an old acquaintance."

"How would he know you were here?"

"Well, that's what detectives are good for, tracking people down. If he is who he claims he is, then that explains it."

Puzzled, Ruby looked at him. "How does what explain what?"

"It just does," John answered, smiling. "Now hush. The bishop's getting ready to start the meeting."

He was, and so Ruby, with dozens of questions spinning in her mind, turned to the front and did her best to focus her thoughts upon the Sabbath School meeting. And she did not see at all the man on the back pew whose eyes were carefully averted to the floor, but who knew exactly where she and John Phips were sitting.

Chapter 9

"Magneto's set," Ruby called.

"Good. I'll crank it up."

With several hard turns John cranked the engine of the Oldsmobile until the spark caught. Then, straightening slowly, he moved around and climbed behind the wheel.

"Do you feel all right?" Ruby asked.

"Fine. A touch of rheumatism is all. Must be a storm coming."

"Oh, that couldn't be. Look at this weather, John. It's lovely, far too lovely for a storm."

"It is beautiful," John responded as he swung the automobile out into the street. "No clouds, nothing but this warm south wind. If it weren't for my joints coming apart, I'd say I was wrong."

"Well, let's hope you are. I'm getting too old to enjoy winters anymore."

"Now stop that talk," John declared chidingly. "You're only as old as you think you are. And I'll tell you the truth, Ruby. You don't look any older to me than a fresh-picked mountain daisy."

Ruby smiled wanly. "Johnny, you do say the nicest things. I just wish my son would be a little more tolerant of you."

"Now Ruby, don't be too harsh on him. Willy is a good man who happens to be very worried about his mother and her welfare. You wouldn't want him to be unconcerned, would you?"

"No, I don't suppose I would."

"He's a fine man, Ruby, and you have every right to be proud of him. By the way, what are your plans for him and me?"

"Plans?"

"You know that he's going to push until I'm gone, don't you? He won't let up, Ruby, and you're the only one who can stop it."

"I know," she replied miserably, "and I . . . I just don't know how. I've tried. Oh, how I've tried, but I just can't do it. My hope is that it will just sort of work out."

"Mostly things do," John responded quietly. "If given time."

For a few moments John drove in silence, steering down Merchant Street past Shelly and Thornton General Merchandise, Roberts Brothers Drugs, E. H. Boley Meats and Groceries, and the Chipman Mercantile Company. At Main he turned east, and it was there that Ruby noticed his eyes fasten briefly upon a gray-haired man who seemed busy studying the new outfits behind the window of Studebaker Brothers Wagons, Carriages, Buggies, and Harnesses.

"Is that the man?" Ruby asked quietly. "The one Willy was talking about?"

"It could be. Say, what do you say we go for a drive?"

"A drive?"

"Certainly. On a beautiful day like this, a couple of old spooners ought to do a little sight-seeing. Normally I wouldn't use the Sabbath for such activities, but I don't know if you and I will ever have another Sunday together, and I'd like to make it memorable. What is there that we might see, do you think?"

"Johnny, I'll never understand you."

"Shure and ye will. Ye already do, me garjus wee lassie. Now, where should we go?"

"You already know the Highland Bench, so that isn't—"

"How many roads come off the bench, Ruby?"

"Roads? Well, the one we drove on this morning that crosses the Mitchell Ditch, and another over on the west side of the Bench by the Lehi Ditch. That one also comes into American Fork. Then there's the road up to Alpine, and a road that cuts across the dry farms and through Dry Canyon toward Salt Lake City. Then over by the mountain there's a road that goes into Pleasant Grove. It follows their ditch, too."

"How about up the canyon?"

"Yes, there's a road up there, a pretty good road, in fact."

"But that road is a dead end, isn't it?"

"I'm certain that it is, at least for automobiles. Why?"

"Well, I'm partial to canyons, always have been. But sometimes they're traps, you see."

"Johnny, what is going on?"

John grinned at the woman at his side. "It's a puzzle, isn't it."

"Johnny?"

"Ruby, I'd tell you if I could, but I don't even know all of it myself. Shall we go for a ride up the canyon?"

"Johnny, are you in trouble?"

John smiled thinly. "Ruby, I've lived with trouble of one sort or another for most of my seventy-two years. If I didn't have more, it would be a real surprise."

"What have you done?" Ruby then asked, her voice quiet.

"Done? Why, I've found me the loveliest woman in all the world, and I've fallen end over teakettle in love with her."

"And?"

"And? Isn't falling in love with you enough?"

Ruby finally laughed. "You're a hard man to get information from, Johnny Phips. Let's go for that ride up the canyon."

John beamed and, following Ruby's directions, drove the Oldsmobile into the mouth of American Fork Canyon.

"There has been a great deal of work done up here," John said as they drove up the rough and winding road.

"I'll say. This canyon has been in a turmoil since the first ore was discovered, back in 1870. There was a toll gate back there at the canyon mouth until just four years ago, with the revenue used to keep the road in repair. Teams passed through for fifty cents, buggies twenty-five cents, saddle horses a dime, and livestock five cents a head. I don't know that I ever heard the toll for automobiles."

"Likely they never had one pass through the gate," John declared.

"No, I don't imagine they did. That building over there is the power plant built by the Graff Brothers. There's a new one going in higher up, and both will supply power to us through the Utah County Power and Light Company."

"Is that a railroad bed?"

"It is, or was. Eric Adamson told me that back in 1870 the Miller

Mine was discovered on Miller Hill. The Aspinwall Company, which bought the mine, built this railroad in 1872 to haul supplies in and ore back out. The terminus was up the canyon at Deer Creek, though they intended to go higher. At first the cars were hauled up by locomotive, and then sent down the grade under power of gravity. During the last year or so of operation, the locomotive was sold and mules were used to haul the cars up the canyon. I never could determine which was the noisiest, mules or locomotive."

John smiled. "It must have been a profitable mine."

"It was, until 1878, I think. Then the ore ran out and the tracks were torn up. The old bed is still down in the river bottoms below my home."

"So this was a mining canyon."

"Was, and the way I hear tell, still is. Once there were even a couple of communities up here—Deer Creek and Forest City. Other than a boarding house and some charcoal kilns, I don't know what was at Deer Creek. Forest City, on the other hand, had about one hundred and fifty inhabitants. Mr. Alder frequently did business with the principal mines and sawmills in the area. It was a rough town, though, and he didn't usually let me visit there with him.

"There was an epidemic there, too. Several people died, including the three Birk children, whose parents ran the saloon. Because of the cemetary, the entire area has since become known as Grave Yard Flat."

For a time the only sound was the automobile grinding its way up the canyon. John drove, and Ruby relaxed, her memories of the canyon filling her mind.

"A few moments ago we passed Dance Hall Cave," she explained. "I went there once with Mr. Alder and had a grand time. But it was difficult to get to, and as a business enterprise it faded away."

"Is that the road up there?" John asked as he looked up the steep side of the mountain.

"Yes. That cut is called Van's Dugway. Sometime, years back, a fellow named VanHousen was hauling mail up here when he was killed by a snowslide. He was buried right here, and the dugway was named after him. A few years ago I heard that a flood washed out his coffin, and so he was taken out and reburied in the cemetery on Grave Yard Flat."

"Well, I hope this outfit of yours can make the climb. I drove one of Ford's new Model T's last year, and on grades like that, we had to drive in reverse."

"Why?"

"Well, it's the way Ford's gear ratio is set up. The doggone automobile has more power in reverse than it does going forward."

"I . . . I don't know about my Oldsmobile. I haven't ever driven it up here."

"Neither have I, Ruby lass. What say we give it a try?"

Smiling, Ruby nodded, and so John started the motorcar up the steep cut-bank.

"Johnny, don't get so close to the edge."

"Now, Ruby—"

"I mean it! I'll get out and walk if you—"

"Easy, woman. Easy does it. I won't go off, and coming back down, you can be on the inside and *I* will be the poor, frightened soul looking down into the awful void."

"Johnny, please . . ."

Inching upward, the Oldsmobile finally topped out above the dugway, and both John and Ruby breathed a sigh of relief.

"This is mighty pretty up here," John declared as he stopped the motorcar to let it cool.

"It is. And the air is so fresh that it feels like you can drink it. Why was that dugway so frightening to me, Johnny? I've never been frightened going up it in a wagon."

"Well, wagons go more slowly. Then too, wagons have teams pulling them or holding them back, and animals are notorious for taking care of their own good health. I think we've depended upon them a great deal more than we ever thought."

"And this motorcar has no animals in front."

"Exactly. All we have to trust is a machine, and machines break down with frightening frequency. I don't wonder that you feared, Ruby. I was a mite nervous, myself. By the way, where are we now?"

"I think this is called Dutchman's Flat. Up ahead are the terraces where Forest City was located. Off that way is Shaffer Fork, with all those kilns they used for making fuel for the smelter. On this other side is Mary Ellen Gulch. Up there is where the Sultana Smelter was located, and where Ed Hines still lives. He's been there most as long as the canyon, I think, and he never loses his dream about making his big strike. From what I hear, he's the one who keeps things concerning mining and rich ore stirred up."

"Must be a lonely life."

"Well, the story is that he had a girl in New York but couldn't afford to marry her. He came west, and years later when he went back for her, he found that she had given up on him and had become a nun. I heard he finally married and has a family, though I won't swear to it. There's also a story that during a terrible storm up here, his wife became so frightened that her hair turned white in a single night."

"Must have been quite a storm."

"They do get bad up here. One night Mr. Alder and I were in an electrical storm up in Mineral Basin that I would have sworn would kill us all. That it didn't, I still believe, was a miracle."

"Johnny, why do you keep looking behind us? Is that man following you?"

"I doubt it," John replied. "I've just been looking for . . . uh . . . what is all that mining up there called?"

Ruby looked at the old man, wondering why he was so secretive. He was a master at changing subjects, and she didn't want them changed. She wanted to know what was going on. Only . . .

"That's Miller Hill," she answered reluctantly, "where it all started back in 1870. Over there is the Blue Rock area, and this is . . . Well, that's funny. I can't remember what this is called. I know that there is ore all around us, though."

"What sort of ore do they mine here?"

"Well, gold, of course, and lead and silver and some zinc. Miller's Hill was so rich when they first started mining it that they used oxen to plow the ore right off the surface. Jacob Beck, one of my neighbors, was working the oxen one day, dragging timbers as I recall, when he was gored in his cheek. He still carries that terrible scar.

"Up there near the top of Miller's Hill is a solitary grave, and in that grave lies a wonderful man, George Tyng. Would you like to hear about him?"

"Faith an' I would. Any time I can hear yer garjus voice, Ruby lass, I enjoy it. Yez keep talking, and I'll keep listening."

Ruby giggled. "You know, you do that Irish accent very well, especially for an American. But you've surely gone and kissed the Blarney stone, so maybe, by right of blarney, you are a true Irishman."

"I mean every word I say, Ruby, and you know it. Now tell me about this Tyng fellow."

"All right," she smiled. "He came here in 1899 or 1900 and stopped at the Grant Hotel and livery stable. There he hired Christopher Beck, the owner of the hotel, to pack him up into either Mineral Basin or Miller Hill—he didn't seem to care which.

"Christopher agreed to pack him in for fifty dollars, and so they went. And on Miller Hill, the back side, actually, Tyng started mining immediately. By that fall, he had spent nearly $35,000 and had found no ore in his mine. Then, on the last day of operation, his foreman, Jack Howes, accidentally struck rich lead ore while picking out some rock. Thus Tyng's fortune was made."

"So what happened to him?"

"Johnny, he was a wonderful, generous man. I can't tell you how many people I know who have been helped financially by him. He bought great amounts of produce and dairy products from our local farmers for his miners, and he always paid a dollar more in wages than anyone else around. He was just grand.

"There is even a story that the Mormon Church needed a $5,000 donation. They sent a General Authority down to see him, and Tyng felt that the amount requested was a little steep, especially since he wasn't a Mormon. So the authority told him to go pray about it and ask the Lord if $5,000 was too steep and if it wasn't the Lord himself who wanted the money.

"Tyng prayed, came back to the General Authority the next day, and wrote out a check for $10,000. He said the Lord had told him that he should have been smart enough to listen to the General Authority in the first place. But since he hadn't been, the Lord was teaching him to listen better the next time."

"That's a great story, Ruby. Do you think it's true?"

"I think so. I've surely heard it often enough."

"Well, true or not, it's a great story. So what ever happened to Tyng?"

"Well, the winter of 1905-1906 was a terrible winter, with a great deal of snow. Tyng stayed up on the mountain running his mine, but one afternoon in January, a snowslide slammed into the building where he was working, killing him instantly. His will stated that he wanted to be buried up here on the mountain that he loved, and so there he is. And I don't think a more lovely place could be found. In fact, one day I picked twenty-two different kinds of wildflowers within ten feet or so of his grave."

John sat silently, his mind obviously somewhere else.

"Johnny?"

"I . . . I'm sorry. What did you say?"

"I said I once picked twenty-two kinds of wildflowers near his grave."

"Twenty-two," John replied almost absently. "That's a lot of flowers."

"It was," Ruby responded nervously. She knew John was troubled about something, but she didn't know how to get him to share it with her.

"A few years ago," she continued hesitantly, "Willy brought me back up here, and the ground had been so grazed by livestock that I hardly found any flowers. Now I hear that they don't permit grazing up here."

"So there's a lot of livestock up here?" John questioned, looking around.

"Oh yes. Kitty Nash, mother of Worthy Nash, first brought dairy cows up here back when the first mines were operating on Miller's Hill. Since then there have been thousands of head of cattle and sheep summered on these mountains. This is wonderful graze. I think that . . . Johnny, what on earth is wrong?"

"Wrong?" he asked, turning to look at her.

"Yes. You ask questions, but for the past few minutes your mind has been a thousand miles away. What is it?"

"It . . . it's nothing. I just . . ." John Phips looked at the woman by his side. "You know," he declared, changing the subject again, "I think it's time that we started back. You ready?"

Ruby nodded, so John turned the motorcar around, and for a time they rode in silence, working their way down to the downslope of Van's Dugway.

"Here we go again," John said, and with not a word from Ruby he started down the cut. It was not difficult, and John was enjoying the ride when he made a turn around a projecting cliff and suddenly looked through an opening in the trees.

"Now this is what I need," he exclaimed. "Just the stretch of road I have been looking for. Where does that canyon down there at the bottom of the dugway, the one running west, end up?"

"At Silver Lake," Ruby replied. "American Fork, Lehi, and Pleasant Grove recently dammed it, and they are still squabbling over water rights. Meanwhile, lowly Highland, directly in the mouth of the canyon, gets legally not a drop, and some folks, just to drink and water a few head of livestock, have even had to resort to stealing it."

"I thought Brigham Young told the Saints that water was not to be owned."

"He did. Trouble is, cities owning water is different from people owning it, and few cities can be classified as Saints. It has been a long and difficult battle, and it still isn't over. I'm one of the lucky ones, because Mr. Alder dug a well and we were fortunate enough to find plenty of good water. Many of my neighbors didn't fare so well."

"So the Saints fight over water," John mused. "Folks don't change much, do they. Here, it's water; in Ohio and Los Angeles, it's political and economic power; in Colorado, it's ore; in Texas and the Northwest, it's land; in . . ."

Suddenly John spun the wheel of the Oldsmobile and drove the car into a turnout on the steep grade of the road. Levering the gasoline down, he climbed out, stood for a minute while the dust settled, and stretched.

"Do you want to wait in the motorcar?" he asked.

"Where . . . where are you going?"

"Just up into those trees, so I can see the road down below."

"Is he . . . is he . . ."

"Ruby, I don't know. That's why I stopped. Why don't you wait in the car, and I'll be back in a moment or two."

So, while John climbed quickly onto the low, pine-covered ridge, Ruby sat in silence in the idling automobile. She was confused, but more than that, she was afraid. What was John Phips involved with? Why would he be showing such fear?

It reminded her vividly of the days and nights of fear during "the raid," when federal marshals were seeking Mormon polygamists and jailing them as fast as they could capture them. Her brother Jons had finally been caught, and that had been the night when a neighbor had sounded a warning and he had been forced to slip away into the darkness.

She had hated that, for she had loved the man dearly and hated to see him suffer. And now she was feeling all that agony again, for truly had she come to love John Phips, and just as truly did she fear for him.

"Ruby?"

Startled, Ruby spun about to see John standing beside the car, smiling.

"I didn't mean to frighten you," he said easily. "You looked like you were an awful long way off."

"I . . . I was. Johnny, please be honest with me. What is going on?"

John didn't answer. Instead, he got into the car, backed onto the road, and started down the canyon.

"Johnny—"

"Ruby lass, I'd tell you if I could."

"Johnny, this isn't fair."

"I know. It's just that . . . well, Ruby, it has something to do with all those years that I don't like to talk about, all those lonely years when I was dreaming of finding you. They weren't happy years, but still I had to live, to keep going. I did so by accepting various kinds of employment, and all this has to do with some work I did some time back."

"Work? Johnny, did you get on the wrong side of the law?"

"Would you believe me if I said no?"

"You know I would."

"Very well. No, I didn't."

"That's all?"

"It is for now. I just wish that . . . Uh, Ruby, is that creek up ahead the one you called Tibble Fork?"

"Yes," she answered hesitantly.

"Good. Now I know where I am. Can you drive home from Tibble Fork?"

"I . . . I suppose. But why, Johnny? What—"

"I need to walk."

"From *there?*"

"Yes ma'am. And that's all I can tell you, except this: Ruby Alder, I love you. And if I can do it, I'll be back later tonight."

"You . . .you love me?"

"I do."

"Promise you will come back, Johnny?"

"Of course."

"For . . . for me?"

"Well," he grinned, "partly. I don't want to miss that dedication tomorrow morning, either."

Pulling to a stop, John climbed out of the automobile. "Here," he said quietly, "now remember, you don't need to travel full throttle. Take it easy until you're out of the canyon. And Ruby, trust me, please."

"I do, Johnny. I just . . . Oh, please come back. I can't bear the thought of you going away."

But John Phips was already descending the side of the road, and Ruby knew that he had not heard her. And he was limping, limping badly. Once again Ruby cast her eyes at the sky.

Was a storm coming, as Johnny had predicted? Did those high, thin clouds mean something? Was that something else with which she had to contend? How could she do it, when there was so much more to be afraid of?

Afraid. How she despised that word! For so many years she had lived with fear, and now it was back again, clutching her innards in a terrible gripping knot, making her head pound while she watched the man she loved walk away from her.

But no, she wouldn't let it get to her. For Johnny she would be strong. She would go home and wait, and she would do all in her power to ease his life until this terrible thing, whatever it was, had passed.

"That's a promise," she shouted into the mountain fastness where John had disappeared. "John Phips, come back to me, for I will be waiting!"

And with a forced smile upon her face, Ruby Soderberg Alder started the automobile and lurched uneasily down the narrow mountain road back to town.

Chapter 10

"Mother, I swear it! Grandma let that old man *kiss* her last night right there on her porch. Ferd and I both saw her."

Allyson Alder stopped speaking, but her wide eyes spoke volumes.

"We've talked about it all day, Mother, and after seeing Grandma sitting so shamelessly with that old man at church today, we decided that we needed to tell you and Father what we saw."

Flora Alder stood still, looking from her seventeen-year-old daughter, Allyson, to her neighbor Ferdinand Burroughs, who at the moment was Allyson's steady beau. Then she looked back to her daughter.

There was no question about it. The two were serious about their accusation, and Flora didn't know what to do. In her mind she pictured her mother-in-law, and no matter how she twisted things around, she could not imagine Ruby kissing that old man. Yet Allyson had never deceived her, and the look on Ferdinand's open face told her that Allyson wasn't beginning a career in lying just yet. So that left things about as they appeared. Ruby Alder had allowed the old tramp who was staying in her barn to kiss her.

Flora thought of her husband, Willy, and wondered what he would do when he learned of his mother's indiscretion. Poor Willy. He was very conscious of his position, and this would cause him great discomfort. But even more, he was worried about his mother, for he had seen just such indiscretions destroy many others before her—lonely women who fell in love with men who were only after their money, and who ended up with broken hearts and empty bank accounts as the result of their misplaced love.

But why would Ruby fall in love with such a man? Flora cast about in her mind, and for the life of her she couldn't imagine an answer.

Senility?

No, hardly that. Ruby was somewhat feeble, but certainly that didn't apply to her mind.

Desire for romance?

Perhaps, but in the ten years since Henry Alder had died, there had been no sign of that, ever. And there *had* been opportunities for Ruby, plenty of them. Many times she had been approached by one or another of the lonely male citizens of the community, and always Ruby had rebuffed their amorous advances.

So why now?

Flora's thoughts were interrupted by the harsh ringing of the new telephone. She jumped a little just as she always did when it rang, and with a tight smile she walked to the wall.

"Hello," she shouted, holding the phone to her ear and straining to get her mouth near the too-high mouthpiece. "Oh, hello, Willy dear. What? You *what?* No . . . no I wasn't questioning you, I just can't hear . . . Oh, very well, that will be fine. Good-bye, darling."

Flora hesitated an instant after her husband had hung up, and then with a mischievous smile she spoke again into the speaker.

"And good-bye to you, Effie, my dear."

There was a gasp and a hurried click, and with a satisfied smile Flora placed the phone back in its cradle. Effie was a wonderful operator, but nosy, terribly nosy. Do her good to know she wasn't fooling anyone.

Turning away from the telephone, Flora walked back to Allyson and Ferdinand.

"Well?" Allyson asked.

"Well what?"

"Well, what are we going to do? Are you going to tell Father?"

Flora shook her head. "I don't know, but I don't think so—at least not just yet."

"Why not? Do you think he'll cut her off from the Church?"

"Either that or shoot her," Ferdinand said, speaking for the first time.

"Ferdinand," Allyson stormed, "what an awful thing to say!"

"Aw, I was only funning," Ferdinand mumbled. Then, with a lopsided look that might have been intended as a grin, he spoke again. "Speaking of utterly, Mother's cousin Tom has a cow who grins every time she walks through tall grass."

"What? Ferd, I declare, I don't—"

"Yup. She's *udderly* tickled to be there. Har de har har."

Allyson looked helplessly from Ferdinand to her mother. "I swear," she said. "He's got more awful jokes than any two people I ever knew."

Flora smiled. "I don't think it was awful. In fact, I think it was wonderful. Ferdinand, in his own sweet way, is trying to get us to laugh about this instead of treating it so seriously."

Surprised, Allyson looked back at Ferdinand. "Is that true?" she asked him.

"Yup," the boy declared, happy that this out had been so well articulated for him.

"Well, I declare. What a sweet thing to do."

Ferdinand grinned. "Yup. Smooching's supposed to be a laughing, fun-time, feel-good sort of thing. Was it me on that porch, I'd just as soon be left alone to enjoy myself, instead of being hauled off before some bishop."

"Even if that bishop was your son?" Flora asked curiously.

"If I had a son who was old enough to be a bishop, I'd certain sure be legal age to try smooching," Ferdinand declared. "Seems to me by the time someone's as old as Grandma Alder, she ought to be old enough to make up her own mind about what she feels up to doing. And she sure enough felt up to lettin' that tramp feller smooch her a good one. Most made me wish a certain girl was smooching me, seeing how good and fine that smooching looked to be."

"Ferdinand Burroughs!"

"Well it did, and I'll speak my mind about it, too. That one kiss you gave me last week made me wish for a whole lot more, but I can't seem to find the well."

"Well?"

"Yup, the wishin' well where I can throw in my fortune wishing for more of them kisses you promised me after that first one. Reckon I've about give up the search, though. I'm fixing to go join the French Foreign Legion like Pa's second cousin once removed, feller by the name of Martin T. Futzbusket. Like poor Cousin Martin, I'm fixin' to pine my life away with memories of your sweet lips brushing that one lonely time against mine. No sir, I don't blame Grandma Alder even a little. A person's got to enjoy what kissing they can, when they can. Seventeen or seventy, it makes no difference. You just never know when your smooching'll be cut off and your heart tossed out in the dust to wither up and blow away in the terrible winds of loneliness and sorrow while the one you love skips away without so much as a backward glance.

"Puts me in mind of Pa's uncle Zach, who had him a terrible spat with his wife, a mean little woman name of Zinnie. Zach was a big strapping man of one hundred sixty pounds when they had that spat, and for a whole year Zinnie wouldn't talk to him nor kiss him nor even admit that he was livin' with her. When asked about it, Zach would say, 'Treats me as though I am dead,' he'd say, and soon his weight began to drop like flies on a cold night, until there wasn't left of him no more'n enough to hold his shoes down to the floor. He died at about fifty pounds, killed on account of a woman who held back her simple, natural affectionate smoochin' from the man who loved her.

"No ma'am, smoochin' is terrible important for keepin' a body alive and well, and if I can't get any more smoochin' of my own, well, I'm awful pleased that Grandma Alder can."

Allyson, at that prolific speech, turned a bright red, Ferdinand glared at her defiantly, and Flora fought back the laughter that was struggling for release. Ferdinand Burroughs, she suddenly realized, was good for Allyson, who quite often got as uppity as her father, and who quite regularly looked down her nose at the boys who chased after her and tossed their hearts at her feet.

"I . . . I do declare!" Allyson fumed. "Ferdinand Burroughs, just you see if I ever—"

"Allyson," Flora Alder said, placing her hand upon her daughter's arm, "don't you be hasty. Ferd's right, you know. Grandma

Alder wouldn't be kissing that old man if she didn't want to."

"But Mother—"

"No, I mean it. Grandma Alder is a fine woman, and kissing is something very special to her. You can bet your best Sunday frock there is something behind this that we don't know about."

"Well, we'll know when Daddy finds out what Grandma is doing. He'll get the truth out of her."

"Allyson, I don't think your father should know about this just yet."

"But Mother, he's . . . he's her *son*. He ought to know! He can tell her to stop before—"

"What if she doesn't want to stop?" Ferdinand asked.

"Well of course she does! Why, kissing that old man is . . . is *lewd*."

"Then how come that kiss you gave me last week wasn't lewd?"

"It . . . it . . . I mean, I . . ."

"Allyson, your father is still at the ward meetinghouse. He won't be home for maybe another hour. Why don't you and Ferdinand go and see Grandma Alder, and—"

"What? I wouldn't go *anywhere* with this nincompoop."

"Nincompoop, am I? Who was it sneaked up to your grandma's porch when you saw them sitting there? Who was it knocked over that pot of geraniums and broke it in a million pieces? Allyson Alder, I may be a nincompoop, but I ain't a sneaky, clumsy one. Next time I take you anywhere, I'll crate you, just to protect the citizens of this fine community and their valuable property."

"Why, you big oaf. I'll have my father throw you out."

"Ha! He couldn't throw nothing but a fit."

"Says you, you skinny lummox. When Father gets through with you, it'll take fourteen doctors to fix all the things that'll be broke."

"That's broken, not broke," Ferdinand said easily.

"You're a fine one to be teaching grammar," Allyson stormed.

"Yep, massacrein' grammar's my specialty. Now come on. Put a smile on that cute little face of yours and let's go do what your mother told us to do."

Without waiting for an answer, Ferdinand Burroughs took a pro-testing but obviously willing Allyson Alder by the arm and led her out the door. Smiling, Flora watched them go, and she was just turning back into the parlor when the telephone jangled again, frightening her half out of her wits.

"Blasted new-fangled contraptions," she muttered as she strode toward the too-high wooden box. "They ought to put warning lights on them so they don't startle a body so badly. I do declare, this is worse than that automobile Grandma Alder bought last year—peskier, at least. Makes me wonder what will be coming next. Progress and Grandma Alder, it's all trouble with a capital T."

And with that she picked up the telephone and shouted, "Hello!"

Chapter 11

"Grandma, are you home?"

Starting at the voice of her granddaughter, Ruby looked up from the old teakwood box that held the photographs and letters that made up the treasures of her life.

"Grandma?"

"I'm in the parlor," Ruby called. "Come in, dearie."

Carefully Allyson made her way through the darkened doorway, Ferdinand following closely behind her. In the parlor she paused, and Ruby stood and turned on the single electric lamp.

"Hi, Grandma."

"Hello, Allyson. And is this Ferdinand Burroughs? My goodness but you have sprouted, young man."

"Yes, ma'am, so my ma says when she buys me new britches."

"Well, sit down, both of you, and tell me to what I owe this visit."

Allyson seated herself and squirmed a bit with her discomfort, and Ruby almost smiled at the young lady's transparency. Oh how long it seemed since she had been Allyson's age. Yet the memories of those golden years were fresh and brilliant, and she knew without even thinking about it that Allyson was concerned that Ferdinand had placed his arm behind her on the sofa.

"Ferd," she finally whispered. "Don't—"

"Now don't be nervous," Ferdinand responded. "Grandma Alder ain't like my great-aunt Amanda Minerva. No she ain't, not a bit."

"What? What on earth are you talking about?"

"I'm talking about Grandma Alder and my great-aunt Amanda."

"Ferd!"

"Well," the boy smiled, "I am. You don't need to be so nervous about Grandma Alder. With Aunt Amanda, me and my brother Frank always ran and hid when we seed her comin', 'cause she allus kisses a feller and wants him to pick her some berries or something. That's her long suit—berries. I don't reckon she'll be happy in paradise without they've got berries there. And Frank bets there'll be a great old scramblin' amongst the angels, too, to keep from getting kissed. She's a terror, Aunt Amanda is. I'm thankful your Grandma Alder ain't like that."

Allyson stared in disbelief at the sober young man seated next to her. She hadn't an idea in the world what he had been talking about, but already she had forgotten the arm on the sofa behind her, trying to understand.

"No . . . she isn't . . . I think . . . ," she murmured. "I mean, I . . ."

Ruby, quite aware of Ferdinand's ruse and enjoying his loquaciousness immensely, decided it was time to get to the heart of Allyson's errand.

"Well?" she asked again, intentionally not beating around any bushes. "A visit is somewhat unusual, isn't it?"

"Uh . . . yes, it is. But it is Sunday, and I . . . we thought it might be nice to . . . to . . . we just wanted to see how you were."

Allyson did her best to smile, and Ruby returned it instantly.

"Well, how sweet of you" she responded. "I am feeling just fine, though I do notice that I'm not so quick about some things as I once was."

"Quick?" Allyson asked blankly.

"Yes," Ruby smiled. "A year or two ago and I would have caught that prowler who broke my geranium pot. But I'm not so quick now, so I didn't even try to catch you."

With a startled expression, Allyson stared at her grandmother. "You knew?"

"Of course I knew. I heard you gasp when you broke it, I heard you whisper and giggle afterward, and I only know of one person alive who sounds just like you do."

"Ha," Ferdinand laughed, "I told you she would know."

"You did not."

"Did so, and you know it."

"Brother. Next thing you know, you'll be proclaiming yourself the next prophet of the Church."

Ferdinand grinned. "Funny thing you should mention that, Allyson. Once Grandpa Burroughs lost his false teeth, and Ma hauled me in and set me down and told me to trance. I did my best and had me a good snooze and then woke up sudden and says to them, wild-like, 'Seek ye within the well!' So they did it. But they didn't find the teeth. But only a week afterward, when Pa cleaned the cistern, there them teeth was. Grandpa Burroughs says, 'Well, anyhow, Ferd knowed they was in the damp,' he says. So you see, I did know, just like I knowed that Grandma Alder would hit on it being you that broke her pot."

Ruby laughed, and Allyson, finally caught in the mood, relaxed and giggled a little, herself.

"Ferd," she said, "I do declare. I never heard anybody go on like you do."

"Chin music," Ferdinand answered. "Pa says it warms the soul, and I reckon we all have souls that need a little warming."

"That's right," Ruby agreed. "We all need a little thawing out from time to time. Thank you, Ferd, for helping us. Now Allyson, I think you wanted to speak to me of Mr. Phips. Isn't that right?"

Shocked once again, Allyson could do little besides gape at her grandmother. "I . . . I . . . Well, I . . . we had hoped . . . uh . . ."

"Allyson," Ruby asked seriously, "what is troubling you?"

"That kiss!" Allyson finally declared. "Grandma, how could you do that? I mean, he's a tramp, and we . . . I saw you let him kiss you."

"You . . . you did?"

"I did!"

Slowly Ruby smiled. "Well then, I admit it."

"But . . . but . . ."

"Allyson, I love John Phips, and whether a person is seventeen or seventy, love feels about the same."

"You *love* him? That old man, I mean?"

"I do."

"But Grandma—"

"Allyson, may I take you and Ferdinand into my confidence?"

"I imagine so. I—"

"Now you must promise not to breathe a word of this—not until I tell you that it's all right."

"Sounds pretty deep and dark," Ferdinand observed.

"Well, deep, anyway. Johnny and I are old friends. We . . . we knew each other long ago."

"Grandma, why can't I tell this to Daddy?"

"Why?" Ruby said, confused. "Because . . . because . . . Well, because *I* have to be the one who tells him. And I'm just not ready to do that. I want—"

"Grandma, don't tell me any more. I'll have to tell Daddy, and I really don't want to."

"Yes," Ruby agreed instantly. "You're absolutely right. Doing that wouldn't be fair to either you or your father. Instead, let me simply ask you for your help."

"Both of us?" Allyson asked in surprise.

"Oh, my, yes."

"What would you want us to do?" Ferdinand asked.

"Help me to show Mr. Phips a good time. You see, for most of his life he has been alone. He has had no family, and from what little I can learn, few friends. I'd like to make a little of what time he has left, happy. Would you two be willing to help me?"

"He hasn't *any* family?" Allyson asked.

"None that he knows of."

"Oh, how sad."

"Yes, it is. And he's such a fine man, too. He was baptized when he was a child and even served a mission to the eastern United States."

"Then why . . . why is he a *tramp?*"

Ruby smiled wanly. "That is a sad question, Allyson, but I think it's because he has nowhere to go."

"So how did he come to you?"

"I . . . I'm not certain. I know he met my brother Jons down in Los Angeles and got to know him quite well. From what little I can learn, Jons sent him here."

"But why?"

"I think . . . I think Jons was simply trying to get two lonely people together. He did, too, thank goodness."

"You really do love him—Mr. Phips, I mean?"

"Yes I do, Allyson."

"Daddy is convinced that he's some sort of crook, you know."

"I know."

"Daddy also thinks he's after all your money."

"Well, Allyson," Ruby smiled, "there isn't much to get. But he isn't after my money. Neither is he a crook."

"Are you sure, Grandma?"

"Absolutely. He has assured me of that."

"He might be lying," Ferdinand declared quietly.

"Yes, he might. But he isn't, and I . . . I'm not at liberty to tell you why I feel this way. You'll simply have to trust both him and me about that."

"What about the detective that Daddy heard about?"

"Now," Ruby sighed, "that is a hard question. I really don't know. But I know Johnny, and I know that whatever is happening, he isn't at fault. Will you two help me to show him a good time?"

"Daddy might really fuss at us," Allyson stated.

"Yes, he might. But if you get to know Johnny a little better, then you'll be able to help your father come to know him too. I would suggest, for the time being, that we keep this idea between the three of us. Ferdinand, do you have some suggestions for fun things to do?"

"You bet! But I can't afford—"

"Don't worry about money. We'll spend all of mine, and then John Phips for sure won't be after it."

Both Allyson and Ferdinand laughed with her.

"Thank you both for coming to see me," Ruby declared as she rose to her feet. "I'll look forward to 'sparking' with you."

"Me too," Ferdinand agreed instantly. "The sooner and the oftener I can do a little sparkin' with Miss Alder here, the happier my poor, lonely, miserable soul will be."

"Oh, Ferd, how you do carry on!"

"Yes, I do. It runs in the family, too. Why, I recollect the time when Bige Peebles was working for Pa down in the store. Bige was a bad egg, I want you to know. Couldn't stop consuming nefarious spirits, he couldn't, and it affected him something awful. One night he slept out on the wooden sidewalk in front of the store, the sleep of the drunk, if you will, and Pa took and tacked all his clothes down all around. Then when Bige woke up the next morning and tried to get up and couldn't, it scared him 'most to death and he hollered, 'Help! I'm paralyzed.' 'Oh, no you ain't, Bige,' Pa says, 'but you was yesterday.'

"Yes ma'am, I do come from a long line of carriers-on."

The young couple left, holding hands, and Ruby watched them go. They were so carefree, so happy, so unafraid . . .

And with that, Ruby began, very softly, to cry.

Day 4

Monday
October 24, 1910

Chapter 12

The sun was bright in the hazy sky of another incredibly warm October day when Ruby heard the light tap on her kitchen door. Her breath caught, for the tap was not like Johnny Phips's knock. Yet it had to be him! It had to be. She could not bear the thoughts of him not being there.

Until late into the night, she had remained near the window, watching for some sign of movement within the barn. Yet not once had a light shown, not once had she seen the door open to admit Johnny to his sleeping quarters.

Alternately she had prayed, wept, and sat shrouded and silent with memories, thinking of Johnny in every way that she could, trying to understand what it was that he was involved in. She trusted him, implicitly. And yet Willy, who carried the mantle of her bishop, and who was such a conscientious news examiner, was so against him, and so she had to give consideration to that as well.

And what really did she know about the man called John Phips? Actually, little more than he had told her. His entire history might be one long fabrication, a lie gotten up for almost any reason. If it were, then no matter what was happening, she would be the victim.

But no! How could she be thinking these things? She knew Johnny Phips, and she knew that he would never harm her, never—

The tap came again at the door, and with a start, Ruby realized that she was indeed acting older. Quickly she stepped to the door and opened it. And there he stood, smiling and freshly-shaved and Sunday-suited again.

"Johnny!"

"Top of the mornin', me lovely wee lass. And how be yer spirits on this grand and auspicious day?"

"My goodness gracious," she exclaimed. "You're the cheerful one today."

"Ought to be. Yesterday was the Lord's day of rest, today's the day of the big dedication, and I have the glorious privilege of being with you throughout both. Are you ready to go?"

She was, and moments later the two were motoring south toward American Fork.

John drove in concentrated silence while Ruby sat stiffly beside him, wondering. Should she ask him about last night? Would he tell her if she did? She could probably ask, but just as likely she wouldn't get any answers. She had never known a man who could so easily evade sharing information about himself. Still, she ought to try, for she had a terrible feeling that somehow what Johnny was involved in concerned her.

"I hope we're on time, Ruby. If we aren't, then likely we won't get a seat."

"Oh, I must not have told you. I have a seat on the stand, and you've been invited to sit with me."

John stared. "You want me to—to sit on the *stand?*"

"Yes, I do. Right next to me."

"But Ruby, I don't think I should."

"No arguments or excuses, me handsome laddie-buck."

John looked over at Ruby, his eyebrow lifted in surprise at her own bit of Irish. Then he grinned, and a short while later Ruby escorted him to their place under the canvas canopy where the cornerstone dedication ceremony of the Alpine Stake Tabernacle would take place.

"President Chipman," she declared proudly, "I would like you to meet my dear friend, Brother John Phips. Johnny, this is President Stephen L. Chipman, our stake president."

"It's a pleasure, President," John responded nervously.

"It is, indeed," President Chipman declared. "Ruby is a fine woman and has done a great deal to hold the Church together out on the Highland Bench. We're honored to have her with us on the stand this morning. And any friend of hers is a friend of ours."

"Thank you," John declared. "This will be a lovely edifice."

"Yes, it will. We have allocated $80,000 for the construction, and of course that kind of money can pay for almost anything. As a stake, we're thrilled with what this building should do for our people. Excuse me, please, Brother Phips. I must greet these other folks. I do hope you'll enjoy your visit to our stake."

"Johnny," Ruby said then, turning to another man, "this is Brother Henry Moyle, our stake patriarch. He recently gave Allyson a most marvelous blessing."

"That was the Spirit's doing, Ruby, not mine. Will you be with us long, Brother . . . ah . . ."

"Oh, I'm sorry," Ruby apologized. "This is John Phips, Brother John Phips."

"It's a pleasure," John acknowledged, taking the man's hand in his own. "As to how long I will be with you, Brother Moyle, it's hard to say. I'd like to stay forever, but we'll just have to see how things work out."

"Yes, I see what you mean. I think. Have you and Ruby known each other long?"

"It seems like it. In fact, it seems almost like forever," John declared. "Ruby is a remarkable woman."

"That she is. She was a fine Relief Society president, too."

"Johnny," Ruby said as Brother Moyle was interrupted by another group of well-wishers, "I would like you to meet Sister Jemima Durrant. She is our stake Relief Society president. And this is Sister Annie Hindley and Sister Harriet Jacobs, her two counselors."

"Ladies," John said, bowing slightly, "it is a pleasure."

The women smiled and greeted him and seemed more than gracious. Yet Ruby felt that the sisters, and the brethren as well, were deeply curious about John Phips. And there were one or two who gave her looks that were openly unfriendly—even critical.

"You know," Jemima Durrant said with a smile, "you don't look anywhere near like the ogre I have been told you were."

"You were told I was an ogre?"

"Or monster or a thief or who knows what else. People always talk when a stranger moves in, especially if he does it as you did.

Anyway, I'm glad I've been able to meet you, John Phips. I am greatly reassured."

John nodded and watched the woman turn and go, and then for a moment he and Ruby stood together, greeting others on the stand and watching the crowd gather in the congregation before them. John was terribly nervous, Ruby knew, for he fidgeted constantly and did not seem his usual gracious self.

"Johnny," she finally asked, "what is it? What's going on?"

"Ruby, please. I just can't . . . Look, there's William."

Ruby turned and smiled at her son, who approached, then, and took his mother's hand.

"Good morning, Willy."

"Morning, Mother. I see that our Mr. Phips is still with us."

"Yes I am, Bishop," John answered boldly. "How are you today?"

"I am well, but somewhat surprised that you are yet here."

"That has surprised me as well," John replied.

"Well, I wonder about that, sir. It seems, from the pieces of the puzzle I have been given, that you are here for a definite reason, one that has little to do with my mother's cooking. You should be the last one to be surprised by your presence."

"And do you know that reason?" John asked, too quickly.

"No," William answered slowly, "but I am studying on it, and here and there, good friends are helping me. Shortly the puzzle will fit, and I will know you very well."

"It sounds as though you know what to look for."

"I do," William declared, smiling. "Frankly, for Mother's sake, I hope that you are not what you seem. Good day, sir. Good day, Mother."

Without a backward glance, Bishop William Alder strode off to mingle with other dignitaries, and John and Ruby stood silently, the strain between them almost a palpable thing.

"Ruby—"

"John, don't say anything, at least not now. Let's both simply do our best to enjoy the meeting."

"Fair enough. But I do want to speak with you later. I don't think I'm being fair to either you or William."

Ruby, looking at John's downcast eyes, felt a terrible sinking within her soul. What was he going to reveal? What awful calamity was he about to bring into her life? Was Willy correct? Did this man have evil intentions that would break her heart? Did he have a dark past that might destroy her? How could she know?

"Oh, that must be Elder Orson F. Whitney!"

"You know him?" Ruby questioned in surprise.

"No, but from what I've read, I feel as though I know him. I love his poetry, and his four-volume history of Utah is one of the most profound documents I have ever examined."

"You've read all four volumes?" Ruby asked.

"Most of them twice, Ruby. You see, when a man is alone, he has to fill his evenings in one way or another. I just always assumed that my growing, at least for the time being, would have to be in an area other than family life. I reckon maybe I didn't grow enough."

Ruby didn't answer, but she squeezed his hand and did her best to smile. Then quickly she took her seat while her heart ached with the fear of what she felt certain was coming.

The meeting was memorable, and the dedicatory prayer by Elder Whitney was filled with power and had much that to Ruby seemed prophetic.

Elder Whitney had just finished and returned to his seat when John Phips visibly stiffened in his seat beside her. His eyes were riveted upon an area of the congregation near the back, and Ruby could tell that something had definitely upset him.

"What is it, Johnny? Who—"

"Shhh," John whispered. "I think . . . I think . . . Oh, dear. This is going to embarrass you, Ruby, just as William told you it would. Please forgive me for what I am about to do, but I have no choice. I must deliver a message, and there is no other way."

"What? What are you—"

Without answering, John Phips rose to his feet, crossed in front of the astonished presiding officers, and leaned close to Elder Whitney's ear.

Dumbfounded, Ruby watched as Elder Whitney first listened closely and then nodded in response to John Phips's whispered message.

Turning to the pulpit then, John took a deep breath, smiled a disarming smile to the audience, and began to speak.

"Brothers and Sisters," he said, speaking more loudly than Ruby had thought possible, "'tis a beautiful and memorable morning, to be sure. When it was determined that I needed to take a moment of your time today, I was not given a subject. But I have noticed that I am shaking a little as I stand here, and so that shall be my text.

"For a moment, I would like to tell you the story of a young man who was sick of the palsy. The palsy, as you are all aware, is a terrible disease, a wasting scourge. And the palsy, as you know, is strongly hereditary. It had been in his family lo those many years. His father had been sick of the palsy, and his mother had been sick of the palsy. And, in fact, every member of his family had been sick of the palsy. Yes, my dear brothers and sisters, he had had it for years and years, and—*he was sick to death of the palsy.*

"Brothers and sisters, like that young man, I am sick to death of a palsy we all seem to be afflicted with—the trembling instability of our Christian love for each other. Why, the damage we do is the same as if we, this very day, *planted a bomb in the newspaper office and killed the editor.* Or *murdered him within the walls of his own home!* It would be the same thing.

"I feel to say to you that before such a thing be allowed to happen, I would *try to stop the culprits,* be they *a young man* or an *old,* from perpetrating the deed. Yes, and I would *guard both the editor's office and his home* in my efforts, while my associate should *follow them all the way to their hole.*

"Thank you, brothers and sisters, and may the good Lord prosper us that none will die of this terrible form of palsy. Amen."

In absolute silence, John Phips turned, shook Elder Whitney's hand, and then limped back to his seat, a worried look creasing his face.

"What . . ." Ruby whispered, "Johnny, what in—"

"Shhh," he whispered, "the choir is getting ready to sing the closing number."

"But—"

"Ruby, I'll explain later."

With that, John Phips folded his arms and watched with tense expression while the children's choir concluded the services.

Chapter 13

"Johnny," Ruby said while the buzzing of the surprised members of the congregation surrounded her, "I don't understand—"

"Ruby," John held up his hand, "I can't talk just yet. Can you get a ride home with someone else?"

"I think so, but—"

"May I borrow your automobile? Immediately?"

"Johnny—"

"Decide quickly, Ruby. I don't have an extra second to burn."

"You want to take my motorcar?"

"I *need* to. Right now. I'll be back."

"Oh no you don't, John Phips! If you go anywhere else, anywhere at all, it will be with me at your side. Last night took three hundred years or so to pass, and I won't be spending another evening like that, wondering if I've seen the last of you, wondering if you are all right."

"Ruby, this might be dangerous."

"Good. Then let's get started."

John looked at her, his expression guarded. Then he smiled, and Ruby knew that she had won. She didn't know exactly *what* she had won, but she had won something, and that in itself made her feel indescribably happy.

Almost running, the not-quite-so-young couple made their way off the stand. And Ruby heard, as she hurried behind John, the most amazing comments about "that older brother's *wonderful* testimony." She also saw, as she was pulled off through the crowd, the portly form of her son, Bishop William Alder, who was anxiously questioning a hopelessly puzzled Elder Orson F. Whitney.

"I don't know him," she heard the apostle declare quite loudly. "I tell you, Bishop, I never saw him before in my life. But it was an interesting sermon, don't you think?"

"Very interesting," William responded. "But you see, Elder Whitney, *I* am the editor in question, and that sounded very much like a threat."

Ruby saw her son, his face and voice reflecting his confusion and doubt, and then she and John were outside the canvas walls and running through hordes of buggies and wagons and milling teams, trying to get to her automobile.

"It's mighty crowded," John muttered as he ran.

"Is that good or bad?"

"Neither. Just crowded. I hope our hurrying in that Oldsmobile doesn't start all these teams to stampeding."

"Why do we need to be in such . . . such a hurry?" Ruby gasped.

"Because I can't afford to let them get ahead of me," John declared as he reached the automobile and hoisted Ruby aboard.

"Let who?"

"Later. Is the magneto set?"

"Uh-huh."

"Okay, here comes the crank."

Quickly John turned the automobile to life. And then, hurrying as best he could, he clambered up behind the steering wheel.

"Now where—Johnny! Look! There is that man we saw in front of Studebaker Brothers!"

"I know."

"Well, hurry, before he sees us!"

At exactly that instant the man looked over, gazing directly at Ruby and John.

"John," she whispered urgently, "he's looking."

And then, to her amazement, she saw John Phips look back at the man and signal to him with a head nod. Then John pulled the Oldsmobile out and into the dusty street and the hot October sun.

"Grandma?"

Turning, Ruby was surprised to see Allyson and Ferdinand running into the street behind them.

"Grandma, may Ferd and I have a ride?"

"I don't think—" Ruby started to say, when she was interrupted by John Phips.

"Is that your granddaughter?"

"Yes."

John slammed on the brakes. "Climb in," he called loudly. "But hurry!"

They did, and John started the automobile again.

For Ruby, the next half-hour was the most frustrating time she had ever spent in her long life. First they drove madly to the west, pulling off the street directly in front of William's office. Quickly John ordered Ruby and the others out of the car and directed Allyson and Ferdinand to stand together at the rear of the building near the eastern corner. Then he and Ruby stood together at the front.

He didn't speak, and after one or two attempts at speech herself, Ruby stopped talking also. Instead, she watched as the traffic from the Tabernacle rolled past, raising clouds of dust as various sorts of vehicles pulled off the paved main road onto the side streets.

Many people stopped to shop, but John seemed to pay attention to no particular person or group. He kept his eyes moving, and Ruby was certain that if an ant had crawled across the sidewalk, John would have noted it.

"Mother, what on earth are you doing here?"

"Oh, hello, Willy. Johnny and I were . . . were . . ."

"Waiting for me? I hope not. I'm still trying to digest that thinly veiled threat that Mr. Phips made, and I'm not at all certain that I could maintain my temper."

"Then we won't trouble you," Johnny declared easily.

"You already have," Willy scowled. "From this moment, Mr. Phips, I will pull every string I can pull to find out why you are here and to stop you from hurting my mother or any other individual in this community. Now good day to you."

William Alder walked through the doorway of his office, and John and Ruby stood silently as long moments drifted past. Finally, with a muttered "There they go," John took Ruby's hand and pulled her toward the Oldsmobile.

"Time to go?" Ferdinand called from behind the frame office.

"It is," John answered. "Let's hop to it."

Ferdinand and a bewildered Allyson ran to the motorcar and climbed aboard, and within moments the four were speeding north toward the hill and Allyson's home.

"Johnny, what on earth are we doing?"

"Protecting things, I hope."

In frustration, Ruby shook her head. "I don't understand, Johnny. I—"

"You don't need to understand right now, me lovely lass. Just trust me."

So Ruby tried, while the two in the back seat sat very quietly, trying to do the same. Suddenly a horseman came out of a side street and rode for a moment beside them, and Ruby was astounded to recognize the man who had been in the parking lot at the Tabernacle site.

"Johnny, it's him again! I—"

"Ruby, be still!"

Surprised at John's tone of voice, Ruby meekly obeyed. Then she watched in wonder as John and the other man made signs at each other with their fingers. That done, the man galloped on ahead, and with pounding heart Ruby watched him go.

"Is . . . is he the man who has been following you?"

"He's been around me, but not following me."

"He followed us up the canyon."

"Yes. We had to meet. That's where I went when I left you last evening."

"So you and he *are* working together. May I . . . may I ask who he is?"

"Certainly," John smiled. "His name is Frank Burns."

"The name means nothing to me."

"It shouldn't."

And Ruby, completely confused, grew still as John drove in silence toward the Highland Bench.

A horse hitched beside the road began to pitch and buck as they flew past, but another one, standing hip-shot a few yards farther along, merely switched its tail at bothersome flies and the noise. Then, as they reached the bottom of the hill, John pulled close up behind a buggy that Ruby recalled having seen near her son's office.

Without hesitation John squeezed the rubber bulb of the horn, pulled to one side of the road, and passed by the buggy. And he was grinning without mirth as the two men in the buggy came into view and then passed quickly behind them.

"That is a wonderful machine," he mumbled to a wondering but silent Ruby. "The speed comes in especially handy."

Without another word, John drove the remainder of the distance to William Alder's home, pulled off the road in front, and turned to a surprised Allyson.

"Young lady, your grandmother wishes a word with your mother."

Allyson cast a glance at Ruby, who nodded her agreement.

"Would you have her come out in the yard, please? Right now."

Allyson looked blankly at Ruby, who again nodded.

"Mother," she called loudly as she climbed down out of the motorcar and approached the screened front door of her home, "can you come out to see Grandma?"

They all waited a moment, and Ruby sensed that John was nervous. He had not looked behind him, but she knew he was aware of where the buggy was that they had passed. Looking back over her shoulder, she saw that it was coming up the hill slowly, and—

"Hi, Mother."

Flora Alder stepped quickly off the porch. "I was hoping that you'd drop by after the meeting. This must be Mr. Phips, about whom I've heard so much."

"Johnny, my daughter-in-law, Flora Alder."

"I'm pleasured, ma'am."

"As am I. Grandma, would you and Mr. Phips like to stay for lunch?"

"I . . ." Ruby responded, "I mean, I . . ."

"We'd love to do it, ma'am," Johnny answered. "Only today isn't a good day. Now we don't have much time, and I'm going to say a couple of things that won't make much sense. May I have the liberty to speak freely?"

Surprised, Flora nodded, looking carefully at her mother-in-law.

"Good. For the next thirty minutes or so, will you stay out here in your yard?"

"But Will's lunch . . ."

"Only about thirty minutes. Maybe less. Your husband won't be home before then, or at least I don't think he will. Could you and Ruby find something to do so that you will both be very visible?"

"We can weed what is left of the flowers," Flora replied quietly.

"Wonderful. Do that. Just stay outside and be very visible from the street.

"Now," he said, turning to Allyson and Ferdinand, "what do we do about you?"

"Us?" Ferdinand responded. "Why do you—"

"I know. Do the same thing that you did down at Mr. Alder's office. Go stand in the back and just visit together for a little while."

"Grandma, what is going on?"

"Allyson," Ruby entreated, "please do as Mr. Phips asks."

"Yeah, Allyson," Ferdinand concurred. "Let's go."

Holding hands, the young couple hurried toward the rear of the home, Ruby and Flora got busy with the flowers, and John unlatched and opened the side-hood of the Oldsmobile. Then he leaned in as though he were working on it. Seconds later the driver of the buggy pulled off the road about fifty yards away. There he and the man who rode with him sat, silently watching the house.

Ruby, observing them as well as she could without ever looking directly at them, was suddenly filled with an awful feeling—almost a feeling of evil. It was, she suddenly knew, going to be a long afternoon.

Chapter 14

"Johnny, are you certain that taking these youngsters with us is safe?"

"Should be," John muttered. "When they left, those boys in the buggy were mighty perplexed. Just when they thought they had things worked out, something came along that didn't add up."

"You mean us?"

"Exactly."

"And now we'll follow them?"

"Well, not quite. Frank has that job. We'll just sort of follow along behind."

"And that isn't dangerous?"

"Shouldn't be."

"Johnny, who *are* those men?"

"Couple of brothers called the McNamaras, Ruby. Mighty un-savory fellows."

Ruby stared ahead, perplexed. She felt so lonely, without infor-mation or understanding. If only John would be open with her!

"Johnny, did you threaten to blow up Willy's office?"

"Ruby me lass," John sighed, "I was sending out a message. That's all."

"When you shouted?"

"That's right."

"What about your hands?"

"Same thing, Ruby. A variation of Indian sign language. Frank and I worked it out years ago."

"It was he that you were signaling?"

"That's right."

"Why did we go to Willy's office? Or his home, for that matter?"

"You sound like Sergeant Mike Calahan."

"I . . . I do?"

"You do."

"I just want to know—"

John stopped her with a lifted hand. "Ruby, the McNamara brothers work for some evil people within the unions. They bomb places, like the Los Angeles Times offices, that are against union organization."

"And Willy is against union organization," Ruby breathed.

"Exactly."

"Then why don't you tell him?"

"I can't. Not yet. I intended to tell him at the outset, but somehow you and I sort of got in the way, and now he wouldn't listen to me if I did."

"I think you're right, Johnny," Ruby agreed.

"So there's no telling what William might do that would alert them, and it is very important that they not be alerted. They must be captured instead. That's why I have been so quiet about it."

"Well, why haven't they been captured already?" Ruby asked.

"We've tried, several times. We just haven't been able to find them where an arrest would not endanger other people. Nor have we been able to find their hole here in Utah. I hope that is what Frank accomplishes this afternoon."

"Are . . . are you police?"

"No," John replied quietly. "Sometimes, though, I help the police out a little. Now, where do we turn toward Pleasant Grove?"

"I . . . I . . ."

"Two blocks straight ahead," Ferdinand called from the back seat.

"Thanks," John responded. "By the way, son, what's your name?"

"Ferdinand. Ferdinand Burroughs. You'll be Mr. Phips."

"Call me John."

"All right, John, then you call me Ferd."

"Fair enough. And of course you'll be Allyson," John said then, smiling at the girl.

"I am, but I don't understand what is happening here. Is this . . . the getting together we were going to do?" Allyson asked hesitantly.

"Not that I know of," Ruby answered. "Still, we are together, so we might as well take advantage of the situation."

"Why, I do hate that," Allyson fumed, suddenly upset. "I'm hardly ready for that sort of day, and I only just this morning got this tear in my frock mended. If I get another one—"

"Let me see," Ferdinand said as he reached down and examined the mended tear. Then he rolled his eyes and sat back.

"Yep," he declared, "she's mended, all right, but like my pa's Uncle Filbert says of his wife Agnes's stitchery, I'd hate like thunder to reap as you sew."

There was a startled gasp and a solid slap as Allyson attempted to amputate Ferd's leg with her open palm, and Ferdinand howled in mock pain.

"You . . . you imposter!" Allyson stormed. "You should be butchered for a remark like that."

"Butchered?" Ferdinand asked, his eyes wide. "Funny you should mention that. Saturday morning last, Ma went to the butcher and give him a lathering. 'Just how do you explain these pieces of rubber in the meat you sold me?' she asks while the butcher cowers in mighty fear and tremblin'. 'Why,' the butcher says, doin' his best to sound brave in the face of such terrible adversity as my mother, 'I reckon it's just another instance of provin' that the autymobile is re-placing the horse,' he says."

"Oh, Ferd!" Allyson began to storm. But then noticed that both Ruby and John were smiling widely, and slowly she started to smile herself. "That didn't really happen, did it?" she asked then. "I mean, your mother . . ."

"Mother," Ferdinand interrupted while John and Ruby laughed out loud, "why, she's a caution and an honest-to-goodness wonder. So's her mother before her, who is my grandmother, as I allow you'll agree when you hear. I like 'em. But Pa, he can't take Grandma for no more'n two hours in any six weeks, he can't. So April last, when Grandma comes to visit, Pa takes about all the vexation his constitution can stand up to. Of course, Grandma was awful cross, and she seemed set on staying most of forever, so Pa, he got desperate and put a wad of cotton in Grandma's ear trumpet so's she couldn't hear anything, and she thought she was going plumb deaf and left that very day for home to see her doctor. Pa, he's a caution too, as I allow you'll agree."

Now all the inhabitants of the Oldsmobile were laughing, and Ferdinand was enjoying himself so much that even he smiled, at least a little.

"And speaking of folks being a caution," he drawled as the automobile sped along, "my uncle Adoniram Huckstressor was a caution, too. He was a farmer and a hard-shell Baptist preacher. Once when Mother says, 'Uncle Ad is a power,' Pa says, 'Git out, you don't mean power, you mean pow-wow-er.' That made Mother pretty mad, I'll tell you, though Uncle Ad does filibuster considerable. He's close with a dollar, too, awful close. One time he went into a hardware store to get a tin cup, and after he'd looked careful at several, he says, 'How much is this one?' 'Nickel,' says the storekeeper. Then Uncle Ad says, 'I s'pose you make the usual reduction to the clergy?'"

All laughed harder than before, and Ferd went on.

"Tell you more about Uncle Ad," he said. "One time winter last he got awful mad at a church meetin' because things didn't go his way, and he stomped out yellin', 'My hands is clear! I wash my skirts of the whole matter, and I won't be back!' he says. Then, outside, he found he'd forgot his specs, and he had to sneak back in and get 'em, with everybody snickerin' up their sleeves. I reckon he felt purty cheap, he did.

"Uh . . . where we going, John?"

"Only for a ride, son. We're following that fellow on the horse. Sounds like quite a family you have there."

"Yep," Ferdinand stated. "Plumb crazy. Fact is, last time Grandma came to visit, Pa caught her out of her chair and down on her knees washin' and scrubbin' the floor. 'Mercy!' Pa exclaimed when he saw her. 'Have you gone off your rocker?' he asked. Reckon maybe all us Burroughs have.

"Why, I recollect the time—"

"John," Ruby interrupted, "I haven't seen—"

"They're somewhere up ahead," John responded quietly. "Are we in Pleasant Grove City yet?"

"Matter of fact, we did just enter the city limits."

"Must be something going on here," John mused. "Look at that crowd."

"I haven't the slightest idea what it might be."

"I hope that Frank's close enough," John continued. "If those two birds get into that crowd, they'll abandon that buggy sure as rain falls down. Faith, me garjus lass, and that'll be a haythun disaster."

Suddenly Johnny whipped the automobile around, neatly spilling Allyson into the lap and arms of the pleasantly surprised Ferdinand Burroughs.

"I . . . oh . . . I didn't mean . . ." Allyson stammered as she righted herself.

"Think nothing of it," Ferdinand grinned as he helped her, "for I will. Fact is, I won't be thinkin' of nothin' else."

Pulling off the road, Johnny climbed slowly to the ground. "Sorry to do this, folks, but I'll be back momentarily."

Ruby watched him walk away, his limp noticeable, his shoulders stooped.

"Mighty mysterious, ain't he?" Ferdinand declared.

"Mysterious?" Allyson questioned. "Haunted's a better word. I get the jitters just thinking about what might be going on."

"Jitters? Allyson, I've got me a cousin name of Alphie Jitters Montooth, and one day he says to me, 'Ferd,' he says, 'I won't never be sold down the river—'"

"Ferd, not now! For goodness sake, don't you *ever* run out of relatives?"

"Well, relatives are a relative thing, Allyson. For instance, Pa's got this great-great-uncle whose grandson's nephew's daughter was my kissin' cousin a year or so back at this family ruination we held. I knowed we was related, but she could lay a smooch on a feller quicker'n Mother slappin' my hands out of her cookie dough. She layed a few on me, long ones that like to curl a feller's toenails, and I most got addicted. Then the ruination ended, she went one way and I went another, and I like to have expired from lack of social nourishment. Standin' aside for you, she set up the best anatomical juxtaposition of two ollicular muscles in a state of semicontraction that I ever saw. So like I was saying, relatives is a purely relative thing."

Allyson rolled her eyes in dismay, and Ruby smiled at her. "First time," she said, "that I ever heard a fellow out-talk a girl with just plain jabbering."

"Oh," Ferdinand said, "she generally gets the upper hand, though I warn her she ought not do it too often. Ma's cousin Stella always got the upper hand, too. But she ended up like the Greek soldier name of Ajax, defyin' the lightning bolts of matrimony to the day she died—"

"Well, there comes Mr. Phips," Allyson declared, cutting Ferdinand off at the verbal pass. "He doesn't look very happy, either."

"Either that or he knows that he's lost his chances with Grandma Alder," muttered Ferdinand. "He's certain stuck on you, ma'am."

"Do you think so?" Ruby asked quickly.

"No doubt of it, no doubt at all. I've seen gents that were stuck before, but never one that was stuck quite so deep. Fact is, there was this fellow worked for Pa, name of Fester somethin'-or-other, and he had him a cute little girl name of Gertrude P. Pennybottom, and he says to Pa one day, he says . . ."

Ferdinand rambled on, but Ruby stopped listening, her attention focused on John Phips.

"Confound it!" John muttered as he climbed into the car.

"You mean . . ."

"I mean he lost them in that crowd. How could Frank have been so clumsy?"

"Now what?"

John Phips looked down into the gently inquiring face of Ruby Alder. "Now I don't know, Ruby. I reckon all that is left is to search them out and hope that we get lucky. Now let's get you home. I imagine that you've had enough chasing for one day."

"Or one lifetime. I just wish—"

Only John Phips wasn't listening. Instead, his mind was back on the men he had followed, and as Ruby listened, she heard him muttering under his breath.

"Dern!" he fumed. "Now what am I to do? Alder will be bombed, and I can't . . . I can't . . . Holy Michael O'Murphy, why does it have to be *him* who writes those editorials?"

"Johnny . . ."

John looked down at her, closed his mouth abruptly, and only then, as he started the Oldsmobile back onto the road, did Ruby become aware that, in the back sat, Ferdinand Burroughs was still telling his stories.

Day 5

Tuesday
October 25, 1910

Chapter 15

"Johnny," Ruby called from her back door, "there's a call for you on the telephone."

John, just finishing milking the cow, looked up in surprise.

"For me?" he said.

"Well, that's what Effie says."

Slowly John made his way out of the corral, his rheumatism slowing his walking. At the rear door he stamped the dirt from his shoes. And then, removing his hat, he stepped inside.

"There's surely a storm coming somewhere," he said as he eyed the wooden telephone box on the wall. "Who is it? Do you know?"

"Effie," Ruby called up into the mouthpiece, "who is it?"

For a moment she listened, and then she turned back to John. "Jake? Does that make any sense to you?"

John smiled. "Enough. I'll take it."

Reaching out, Ruby almost handed him the earpiece, but then she suddenly drew it back and turned back to the mouthpiece.

"Thank you, Effie. Mr. Phips is here, so would you please get off the line?"

There was an abrupt click, and with a smile of satisfaction, Ruby handed the earpiece to John.

"Yes?" he questioned, speaking quietly.

Ruby walked away as he spoke, but she could not help but see the concern that appeared on John's face. Something was troubling him, and Ruby was certain it was serious.

Oh, if only she could help! If there were only some way that she could ease the burden that John was carrying. But she could not imagine how she could.

"Bad news?" she asked when John replaced the earpiece, doing her best to push her constantly lingering doubts from her mind.

"No, not exactly. I'm just not certain what to do. I've spent since early this morning doing all I know how to do, to track those birds down and to protect William's office and his home. But I can't find them, Frank Burns can't find them, and neither one of us is effective at protecting Will Alder. I just.wish he would listen so we could tell him what he's up against."

"Could you and Frank go in and see him?" Ruby asked.

"We might could. We've talked about it off and on all day, and we both made a mistake. We should have gone to him first off, before you and me and a whole lot of personal ancient history got all mixed up in it. Now the poor man is so caught up in worry about what I seem to be doing to you that he won't even consider listening to me."

"I don't think that little speech yesterday helped either," Ruby said sadly.

"No," John agreed. "That's another in a long line of my mistakes. I didn't think Frank Burns was watching me, so I had to verbally get his attention and send a message that way. It has worked for us before, at a couple of rallies, and so I thought it would work again. I never even considered that William might think it a threat. Ruby, I'm just getting too old for this sort of thing. I think maybe I'd best—"

The telephone jangled loudly, and both John and Ruby jumped as if they had been shot. John smiled sheepishly, and Ruby smiled back and then took the call.

While she spoke, John stood at the window, staring off into the distance. With half her mind Ruby continued to worry about him, and with the other half she did her best to listen to Allyson.

"Yes," she answered. "It might work, but I haven't . . . Are you *sure*, Allyson?"

Her granddaughter responded, and so with a smile and a promise, Ruby hung up.

"Ruby, I think I ought to leave," John said.

Startled, and with a terrible pain quickly expanding within her, Ruby stared at the old man.

"L-leave?"

"Yes. This has been wonderful, and you'll never know how

much it has meant to me. But things are not working out like I had thought, and I don't want to get you caught in anything that might bring you any more hurt and sorrow. You've had enough of that from me. Besides, this thing is getting out of hand, and I don't know if I have the strength or the intelligence to stop it. By leaving, I will make certain that you, at least, will be protected."

"That . . . that was a nice speech," Ruby declared quietly.

"Well, it was a sincere one."

"But misguided. Johnny, if you have been honest with me, then nothing that could happen, absolutely *nothing,* would cause me greater sorrow than your departure."

"Ruby—"

"Johnny, I mean it. I couldn't take being left alone—not *again.*"

John Phips sighed deeply and then sat down in the old horsehair rocker, where he continued to stare off into the distance.

"Ruby, I really don't have a choice, especially now. I've got to leave you. But before I do, I think I owe you an explanation about these past few days. Like you said, I owe you a little honesty."

"Johnny, *please.* I don't think I can stand it."

Tears were welling up in Ruby's eyes, and John quickly looked away. Ruby didn't know if it was because he was unable to stand the sight of her foolishness, or if it was because he didn't want to see her hurting. So she tried to stop crying, but the harder she tried, the less able she was to do so.

"Ruby," John finally declared, "I can't help it! I'm only thinking of you. If I haven't been totally open with you, it was to protect you. The feelings I have expressed for you, however, are open and more honest than anything else I have said or done in my entire life. And that's why I must leave. I can't bear the thought of hurting you, of causing you more pain. Ruby, sweetheart, with all my heart I love you! That is why I must go."

"No, you *don't* love me, John Phips!" Ruby snapped through her tears. "Not if you leave! Men always use that old line as an excuse for getting out of . . . of their responsibilities!"

"Ruby, people could die. *You* could die."

"Johnny, I'm going to die anyway. I'm an old woman. My body aches just like yours does, and until you walked into my yard and started chopping my wood, I was anxious to get my dying done with. Now I don't want to die, unless I have you beside me, and then I'd like to put it off for another seventy-odd years. But I guarantee you this, John Phips—I'll die a lot sooner if you walk out that door than I will for any other reason."

"Ruby me lass, you don't understand."

"No, Johnny, *you* don't understand. I may not understand all of what is going on, but neither do I think it can be solved by your leaving. To me, what is important is that I want to be with you. Now please stop talking about going away."

John stopped trying to explain, and for several moments the two were quiet, John thinking and Ruby sniffing and drying her tears.

"That was Allyson on the telephone," she finally said softly. "She and Ferdinand have invited us on an outing tonight."

"An outing?" John replied absently, his thoughts obviously elsewhere.

"Yes, but I won't tell you about it unless you pay attention to me."

Slowly John's eyes focused and turned to Ruby. "You know," he said quietly while a smile grew upon his face, "I think you're *better* looking than those Gibson girls. I especially like your blue eyes— how you look at me from behind them."

Ruby blushed. "Oh, stuff and nonsense. Shows how much you know about anything. My eyes have cataracts, and I can hardly see you at all."

"You can't fool me," Johnny teased, grinning. "I know, O faint-hearted one, that you have hardly been able to keep your eyes off me."

"I wish I could *really* see you," Ruby teased back. "It'd serve you right, having all your false hopes blasted so thoroughly and so quickly by my telling you what I could see. Now what about that outing?"

"What outing? I don't recollect—"

Ruby sighed. "John Phips, I *knew* you weren't listening. Now pay attention, for I won't say this again. Allyson and Ferdinand have invited us on an outing with them tonight, and I'd like to go."

"What . . . what do they have in mind?"

"Well, if you had had a day, we were thinking of going to Salt-air."

"Isn't that a resort up on the Great Salt Lake?"

"It is. There are games to play and a roller-coaster that you wouldn't get me any nearer to than a hundred acres of poison ivy guarded by hornets. And, of course, folks go floating in the lake."

"Well, we can't go there, so what do you have in mind now?"

"Do you mean that you'll go?"

"Only if we can shut that Ferdinand kid's mouth for the evening."

Ruby laughed. "Maybe he's out of relatives."

"Not that boy. I've a hunch most of those relatives were born in the fertile but twisted valleys of his own warped brain."

"Johnny, that's awful!"

"So are his stories."

"But you laughed."

John grinned. "I know. Shows what an old fool I've grown to be. Ring 'em up on that telephone contraption, and let's get on with this grand tour."

Ruby picked up the telephone and took hold of the crank, and then she paused.

"Should I invite Willy and Flora?" she asked.

"Why not?" John grinned. "Flora seemed to like me, and given most of an evening, maybe I could convert Willy."

"Give him time, Johnny."

"That's easy to say when you have it, Ruby. Unfortunately I don't."

"Maybe you have more than you realize."

"And maybe we *all* have less."

Ruby sighed. "Well, you don't mind if I ask them, do you?"

"I surely don't. And by the way, me garjus wee lass, I really *do* like your eyes."

Chapter 16

Rarely had Ruby enjoyed an evening more. Willy and Flora didn't go, but John and Ferdinand and Allyson did, and the four of them had more fun than she could even imagine. They went for a ride, and as they rode they sang such favorites as "Come, Josephine, in My Flying Machine," "Bird in a Gilded Cage," "You're a Grand Old Flag," "My Wife's Gone to the Country, Hurrah! Hurrah!" and "Shine On, Harvest Moon," a song made famous by Nora Bayes and Jack Norworth.

Later in their ride they drove west toward Lehi across the dry farms, with Ruby explaining the history of the Orrin Porter Rockwell tavern site, located just north of Lehi; John telling a few whaling stories from his life at sea; and Ferdinand continually regaling the group with tales of his "pestiferous and nefarious" relatives.

"Oh, my hair!" Allyson gasped as a particularly heavy gust of wind slammed into the southbound automobile, tossing her hair even more than it had already been tossed.

"Hair?" Ferdinand asked, while both Ruby and John immediately began laughing. "Hair, you say? Well, folks, let me tell you about Mother's Uncle Tom's cousin, fellow name of Beezum Tweedie. He's a professor, teaches penmanship at some high-falutin' college school, and he knows Shakespeare better'n old Mahomet knew the Koran, or so Pa says. But ain't he a hairy one, though. Once him and a fellow name of Frank Mendenhall was doing Brutus and Cassius wrapped up in sheets in Liberty Hall up in Bozeman, and when Beezum says, 'Here is muh dagger and here muh naked breast!' Pa hollers out, 'Get a shave, Prof, so's you won't be a liar.' Well, it pretty nigh busted up the show."

"Should have just stabbed him in the back," Allyson giggled.

"Oh, my, no," Ferdinand declared, shaking his long, serious face. "That wouldn't have worked none either. Old Beezum had more hair on his back than he had in front. Pa always allowed Beezum was just some poor kidnapped ape that somebody'd hauled up from Africa and shaved a little off the face of.

"But faces? We got two in our family that are more than regular famous, if you know what I mean. The first belongs to Aunt Phoebe, who married up with Mother's brother Jed, who is an awful good singer and who used to travel with Doc Lighthall. He's handsome, too, I think; but Aunt Phoebe ain't very. Mother says she used to be awful pretty till after she got the rheumatism so bad, but Pa says he guesses she must of had it before ever he saw her.

"Pa says she went to a party one time down to Nephi with Uncle Jed, where they was givin' a prize to the one who could make the most homeliest face, and when she walked in the judge walked right over to her and give her the prize. Aunt Phoebe says, surprised-like, 'Why, I ain't even begun yet.'

"Aunt Phoebe sings too, but let me tell you, she's got a voice what's a terror to snakes and all forms of small rodents, and I don't want to talk about it, either.

"The second famous face belongs to the husband of Pa's sister Elviry, fellow by the name of Alvy Freemantle. Now there's a pair, Alvy and Elviry, but of the two, Alvy's got the hardest mug. He was a lieutenant of artil'ry with President Roosevelt during the last war, and he done real well. Pa says the reason why is 'cause of his looks. Pa says, 'Why, if I was a Cuban and seen that expression onto Alvy's mug and him a comin' at me, I wouldn't only hit the high places during my departure,' he says."

By then John and Ruby were holding their sides with the droll humor of the lanky youth named Ferdinand Burroughs. Allyson didn't see all the humor that her grandmother saw, but she smiled and laughed with them anyway, and more and more she was becoming impressed with her young neighbor.

"And speakin' of soldiers," Ferdinand continued, "there's Winfield Scott Zachary Taylor Peebles, Mother's cousin. He was named for two old heroes, Revolutionary War I think it was. Anyway, he could always think of the grandest and noblest things to say. Once when he was in the war, an officer got killed, and they put Cousin Win in his place, so that's how he got to be a corporal. First thing he says was, after whoever it was appointed him to his place, 'Boys,' he says, 'if I fall in this day's battle, march over muh dead corpse just as you would that of a common private!'"

"Humble," John declared.

"Absolutely."

"Especially for a private."

"Correct," Ferdinand continued unabated. "And just hearin' the word *private* reminds me of the twins, Abner and Freddie Spinks, who belong to the youngest daughter of Pa's oldest sister's first husband—"

"Say," Ruby interrupted, trying to stop the ubiquitous flow of verbiage splashing forth from behind her, "wish we were closer to Samuel Wagstaff's or George Jacklin's homes."

"Wh-why?" John asked through his laughter.

"They make molasses, and I could sure do with a molasses sandwich to feed poor Ferdinand. Only thing I can think of that would hold his mouth closed.

"Say, all of you," she declared then. "I've an idea. A year or so back the Ramsey Brothers remodeled the motion-picture house, and I haven't been inside since. Their equipment is good, or so I've been told, and they even have a player piano, so it never misses any notes. Should we see a motion picture?"

All agreed, and the next hour was spent watching the latest in cinematic adventure and romance in the Lyric Theatre. Once the picture ended, they walked north to the Apollo Hall, which had been operating since 1903. It had a spring floor, the first of its kind in the state, and was owned by Joseph J. Jackson, Thomas E. Steele, and associates.

There they danced until Ruby thought she would surely drop, and until John finally did.

"Can't do any more," John moaned as he led Ruby to the side and out into the darkened foyer. "I might have been young once, but the way my leg's carrying on, it's been a spell."

"Your leg," Ruby argued as she limped to the open door, "can still dance circles around mine. After tonight my varicose veins will have varicose veins on them."

"Those two inside don't seem bothered."

"Well, young love is blind to pain as well as to almost everything else."

For a time they sat in silence as Edison's marvelous talking machine ground out another dance inside. Then, as the sound died and Allyson and Ferd talked with the half-dozen other couples out on the floor, John spoke again.

"It's been a wonderful evening, Ruby. Thank you for sharing it with me."

"Johnny, the pleasure has been mine. You've been such a gentleman."

"Well, maybe I've learned a little in the last fifty years. Faith and I shure needed to."

"Johnny, forget that, will you?"

"I wish I could, Ruby me lass. I wasn't much of a man . . ."

"John Phips, you're a fine man, and I appreciate how you have treated me, more than you can know. Why, as simple a thing as that fifteen-minute break you gave me a little while ago did wonders for my tired old body."

John, his eyes again distant, did not respond, and Ruby felt herself wondering again, wondering.

"Maybe you and I can get a moment to sit down together with Willy," she suggested, trying to get him back. "If we go in together, certain of ourselves, maybe we can clear all this up."

"I . . . I don't know. I—"

Whuuuumph!

The muffled sound of the explosion was nowhere near so noticeable as the shaking of the dance hall, and for an instant everyone froze. Then, with a groan, John Phips limped hurriedly out the door and down the steps.

"Johnny, what is it?"

"Willy's office! Stay here."

"Willy!" Ruby cried as she ran after the rapidly limping John Phips, "not my son . . ."

"Confound it all," John was muttering as he hurried toward the small office where William Alder did his writing. "I *knew* I shouldn't have listened to them! If I'd just done what I felt . . . Oh, I hope he wasn't in there. Why did I pick tonight of all nights to go off acting like a little kid? Confound it all, if William was in that office . . ."

The office, when they arrived, was surrounded by people. Or at least what was left of the office was surrounded. A little fire still burned here and there, but the blast had been of sufficient force to literally dismantle all of the building but the foundation.

"Faith," John muttered. "The murderin' whelps must've used more blastin' powder than those Cuban lads lit off under Admiral Dewey."

"Willy?" Ruby cried. "Oh, Willy . . ."

"Ruby, honey, you stay here!" John ordered sternly, ignoring her pleas.

"But Johnny—"

"Please don't argue! I'll find out about Willy, and then I'll be right back. I promise."

"Johnny, please hurry. I must know about Willy."

Fighting the fear that filled her, Ruby stood with tear-streaked face, watching as John limped into the rapidly gathering crowd. Her mind whirled, and desperately she filled her mind with prayer, pleading both for Willy and for John Phips, praying that both of them would be all right.

"Well, Mother, are you satisfied?"

With a small scream of surprise, Ruby whirled to face her soot-covered son.

"Oh, Willy," she cried, "thank God you're all right!"

"I am, no thanks to that old man you've been harboring."

"You . . . you mean *Johnny?*"

"None other. Mother, I told you we'd all suffer if you didn't send him packing. Now he's done this, trying his best to murder me in the process."

"No, Willy! Johnny wouldn't—"

"Mother, you don't know that old man even a little. If he'd only been after your money it would have been bad enough. But this! Oh, why did I let you bamboozle me?"

"Where is he, Mrs. Alder?"

With tears now running freely, Ruby stared at Marshal Harvey Hamilton, who now stood beside her son.

"I . . . I don't know . . ."

"Mother, the man's a known criminal, and has been for years! Harvey here has information linking him to the Molly Maguires in Pennsylvania way back in 1877. He was in Telluride in 1902 when Arthur Collins was killed, and three years ago he was in Boise during the 'Big Bill' Haywood murder trial."

"Wh-what? I don't remember—"

"Sure you do. When Haywood was tried for assisting in the murder of former Idaho Governor Frank Steunenberg. That athiest lawyer Clarence Darrow got Haywood off on a technicality, but your John Phips was there just the same.

"Mother, he's a Wobblie and an anarchist, it is obvious that he works for the unions, and it's *more* than obvious what he has done to me."

"Do you know where Phips is, Mrs. Alder?"

"He . . . he went . . . to see if Willy had been . . . Oh, Willy, he didn't do it! I know he didn't!"

"Do you know where he was tonight?"

"Yes . . . yes I do. We went to the picture show and then to the Apollo Hall to dance. We were there when the explosion occurred!"

"Were you with him every minute?"

"Yes, I . . . I . . ."

"Mother, why do you hesitate?"

"I . . . uh . . ."

"He left for a few moments, didn't he!"

"Willy, when a man gets old, or a woman, too, for that matter, they must make rather frequent trips outside."

"How long was he gone?"

Ruby looked frantically at her son. "N-not long. When you're older, those things take longer, and—"

"That cinches it," Marshal Hamilton declared quietly. "Let's go get him."

And while Ruby Alder buried her face in her tired old hands and wept, William Alder and Harvey Hamilton turned and began forcing their way through the crowd surrounding the demolished office, seeking the arrest of one John Phips, "anarchist."

Day 6

Wednesday
October 26, 1910

Chapter 17

Silently the large old man sat on the bleachers, staring out into the moisture-shrouded Wednesday afternoon. The rain fell steadily upon Los Angeles and its environs; but there was little wind, and the man was sheltered by the high, sloping roof that covered the short grandstand, and so did not get wet.

Out in the field a few pigeons wheeled in the downpour, but most of the hundred thousand birds that made up the famous James Y. Johnson Pigeon Farm were in their coops, long rows of hundreds of stacked pens that bordered the feeding field.

In wonder, the man shook his head. He was amazed that so many pigeons could be gathered into one place *anywhere*. And their sole function, which to him was even more amazing, was the laying of eggs that would hatch out into squab, half-grown baby pigeons. Those, served plucked but uncleaned and steaming hot under glass, had become a delicacy and connoisseur's delight throughout the United States and Europe.

Then, too, he was amazed that the place had become such a tourist attraction. Postcards showing the ranch were sold throughout the West, he had read articles on it in journals published as far away as London, and the Union Pacific Railroad had even built a spur to the ranch in order to accommodate shipping and interested tourists.

The old man had never before been here himself, but somehow the thought of a hundred thousand pigeons wheeling overhead didn't excite him, and so he didn't think he ever would have visited the place. That is, he wouldn't have visited if it hadn't been for—

"Howdy."

Turning, the old man looked up into the eyes of an equally old and equally large gentleman, whose mustache was very similar to his own.

"Hello," he responded quietly.

"Mighty foul weather," the second man said as he sat down. "No pun intended, of course."

"Of course. Are pigeons fowl?"

"Well, they smell like it. I can't believe I own a whole farm of 'em. Mighty interesting seeing the unexpected directions a man's life takes."

For a moment the two sat in silence.

"I hear these storms travel all the way inland, clear to Utah," said the second man.

"Is that so?"

"Way I heard it, by tomorrow this one will be punchin' those Mormon folks pretty hard."

"Interesting. You're James Y. Johnson?"

"I am. And you're the legendary Wyatt Earp."

"Some days," the first old man grinned. "The rest of the time, it's too much trouble even to claim I'm related. From what I hear, you've had a similar problem."

The man called James Johnson turned. "You know?"

"Man keeps his ear to the ground, he learns a lot. For instance, I know you're real name's Soderberg, and I know the Feds once wanted you up in Utah. For all I know, maybe they still do. There are many reasons why a man keeps his name quiet."

"You're right."

The two sat silently then for several minutes, listening to the steady drumming of rain on the grandstand.

"Not much activity out there today," James Soderberg finally declared.

"There is if you're looking backward," Wyatt Earp responded quietly.

"Backward?"

"Uh-huh. Into the past."

"Ghosts, you mean?"

"Plenty of 'em."

Carefully then, Wyatt Earp pulled his watch out of his vest pocket, flipped open the cover, and checked the time. "It's funny," he said quietly, "how you and I have been thinking alike today. You spoke of unexpected twists in a man's life, and I've been sitting here thinking exactly the same."

"We do have them."

"That we do. I find it amazing that a few seconds in a seventy-year life-span will absolutely determine the road a man will follow for the rest of it. And those few seconds are no different than any others, so far as a man can see when he's coming up on them.

"See this watch? Two o'clock in the afternoon. Jim, I . . . Do you mind if I call you Jim?"

"Not a bit."

"Good. Twenty-nine years ago today, Jim, in 1881, at precisely this hour, my few life-determining seconds began. It was even on a Wednesday, just like today."

"Was that the famous gun battle at the OK Corral?"

"It sure was. Me, my brothers Morgan and Virgil, and Doc Holiday were involved. All of us had responsibility for keeping the law down in Tombstone. That day we went up against a bunch of outlaws, part of a band called the Clanton band. The ones we fought were Ike and Billy Clanton, Frank and Tom McLowry, and Billy Claiborne.

"Now, you have to remember, Jim, that the fight occurred in just a few short seconds. Still, the entire scene is burned into my mind as though with a branding iron. I'll never forget it as long as I live."

"I don't think I'd like a memory like that, Wyatt."

Wyatt Earp sat quietly, his face sober. "I don't like it either, Jim. I just don't know how to get rid of it. Whenever I close my eyes, I see men dying. I hear gunfire everywhere, I see faces filled with fear or hatred, and I can't get shut of the nightmare."

"Sounds like a regular war you fought."

"It was—a short, deadly little war. The way I've counted it, Jim, there were seventeen shots fired by each side. Three of the five rustlers died, and three of the four of us were wounded. It's still hard for me to believe, but I was the only one who stood up to the fire and came through unscathed.

"But the scars are there, nevertheless," Wyatt continued. "By Christmas of that year, many folks, at least those who read the Tombstone *Nugget,* thought *we* were the outlaws.

"If they'd read Clum's *Tombstone Epitaph,* they'd have read something else. I've memorized it, and I quote: 'The feeling among the best class of our citizens is that the marshal was entirely justifiable in his efforts to disarm these men, and that being fired upon they had to defend themselves, which they did most bravely.'

"Later on, Judge Wells Spicer held an inquest and examination on a murder complaint that had been filed by Ike and Sheriff Behan against Doc and me. Judge Spicer found not only Doc and me, but Virgil and Morgan as well, innocent of all charges.

"But unfortunately it didn't end there. Right after Christmas, Virgil was shot from ambush and maimed for life. Then in the spring, Morgan was murdered, and I suppose Doc and I went on a vendetta—Sheriff Behan and his crooked law machine in Cochise County just wouldn't help.

"Down in Tucson, I caught up with Frank Stilwell, who had helped kill my brother Morgan. After my shootout with Stilwell, Sheriff Behan tried to arrest me for *that* murder. But Behan had been crooked all along, and I paid no attention to the warrant.

"Not long after, I found Indian Charlie, whose real name was Florentine Cruz, and Curly Bill Brocius. They'd both been in on the shootings of Virgil and Morgan. It didn't take me long to give each of them a fatal dose of .44 slugs or Wells Fargo shotgun pellets.

"After that, Sheriff Behan organized his forces and drove Doc and me up into Colorado, and things have just been a continual round ever since. I've run saloons in Colorado, Coeur d'Alene, and El Paso. I even ran a saloon for a time in Nome, Alaska."

"So in all of that you never got wounded?"

"Nope, but I have been shot, though I'm embarrassed to tell you how."

"What did you do? Shoot yourself?"

"Just about. It was when I got careless in a card game up in Lake City, Colorado. I was accused of cheating, took exception to the charge, even though there was some justification for it, and ended up with a bullet in my arm. The other fellow came out way ahead on that deal."

"That must have been a bad day," James sympathized.

"Well, I have had better. But it taught me a good lesson, and I haven't dealt from the bottom of the deck since then."

"I heard you had a tangle with Clay Allison. You don't mind if I mention these altercations, do you? I've heard about them so often and for so long that it's plumb interesting hearing the facts from one who ought to know them."

"I don't mind. But as to facts, my memory's no better'n anybody else's. Still, I do remember Clay, and I did have a run-in with him—him, John Wesley Hardin, 'Rowdy' Joe Lowe, Sergeant King, and Mannen Clemments. This last bunch I met up with in Wichita. I never did have shoot-outs with them, though. Thumping them on the head with my log-barreled Buntline Special, coldcocking or buffaloing, it was called, has always been my style.

"That's how I took out Clay Allison, down in Dodge, right in front of the Long Branch Saloon. I thumped him when he tried to shoot me. Allison was a bonafide crazy killer. He used to ride naked in the streets shooting at folks, and one night he had a knife fight with a fellow in a new grave out on boot hill just to see which one would fill the grave. Clay didn't."

"Sounds like he wasn't much of a Christian."

Wyatt laughed. "He wasn't. But then, Christianity sort of took a back seat in those wild and woolly days. I've often wondered if I'd been a better man had I stayed where the frontier wasn't."

"Well, most of us have regrets, Wyatt. In a fit of anger I left my wives behind in Utah when the Feds put the heat on me for polygamy, and that was seventeen years ago. Now we've drifted so far apart that I don't know if I'll ever even see them again. It's been awful, and I've often wondered the same thing. What if I'd done it different?"

The two men sat silently then, each wrapped in his own thoughts, each consumed with the heavy burden of memories. Finally James spoke again.

"What are you doing now?" he asked quietly.

"Well, I've refereed a prize fight or two, I've looked for gold out in Tonopah, Nevada, and lately I've been guarding bullion for one of the banks here in Los Angeles. They pay me well, and the job's fairly easy. I'm also developing some real estate, and with one thing or another my third wife, Josephine, and I, seem to manage."

"You've had three wives?"

"Yep," Wyatt agreed. "But I've never had a whole passel of 'em all at one time. What's that like, if you don't mind my asking?"

"Oh, I don't mind. It's about like being penned up in the OK Corral for fifteen or twenty years straight, with seventeen shots a minute coming at you—and your own gun usually empty."

The two old men laughed and then grew quiet.

"I guess we all carry our own ghosts," Wyatt declared.

"That we do . . . that we do. Now, what did you want to meet me about?"

"Well," Wyatt responded quietly, "maybe nothing. But it might be something. And if it is, and I don't tell you, I'll be carrying a few more ghosts. That's why I'm here."

"I'm not certain I understand."

"Well, I'll explain. Years ago I worked a freight line from San Bernardino to Salt Lake City. I got to know you Mormons some and made a few friends, and I was always treated well. There was even a bishop once who stood up for me when I was in a bad fix, and he got me out of it. That means I owe him, and since he's long dead, I reckon I owe the Mormons in general. And whatever else is said of me, let it never be said that I have forgotten my friends.

"The other day, playing cards, I heard such a thing as might be of interest to some of your people. That's what I want to pass along."

"So, why did you come to *me?*" James asked.

"Jim, you're the only man I know in Los Angeles who is a for-sure Mormon. Besides, I heard you used to be a bishop, and that other man taught me that bishops can be trusted."

"I was a bishop, all right. As for my integrity, you can hear both sides of that issue. Depends on who you ask."

"As with most of us," Wyatt chuckled. "Anyway, I figure I can trust you. Do you want to take this information on?"

"Well, I'll see. What is it?"

"A crazy deal, if I ever heard one. You remember a couple of weeks or so ago when the *Times* office was bombed? Last night I heard that the fellows who did it are holed up in Utah—place called Pleasant Grove. They've got another job planned up there."

James, his mind whirling, stared at the elderly marshal.

"Do you . . . do you have any idea how important it is to me to receive this information?"

Surprised, Wyatt looked at him. "No. Do you mean personally?"

"I'll say! Wyatt, from what I can learn, those birds are nesting in Pleasant Grove until they can kill my nephew, a fellow by the name of Will Alder. That's their job."

"Will Alder is *your* nephew?"

"Has been since he was born," James countered. "Funny fellow. Stiff as a ramrod, but he is honest, and he does know his facts."

"I know," Wyatt mumbled. "I read his editorials."

"Wyatt, do you know exactly where those men are in Pleasant Grove?"

Quietly, Wyatt considered the question. "Matter of fact, Jim, I believe I do. At least I heard it. Now all I have to do is recollect it. They're holed up on a street name of . . . of *Locust,* in what's called the old Ed Platt home. It's rock, an older home, they say. And it faces the mountains. That's all I heard."

James breathed a sigh of relief. "Wyatt, I'm beholden. I've been worried about my nephew, and this information just might save his life. I'll send a telegram right away."

"Hope it helps, Jim. I've been mixed up in a little bloodletting in my day, but I don't hold with out-'n-out, indiscriminate murder. Bombs do just that, killing anybody nearby. Like I say, I don't hold with that at all."

"Neither do I. Want any squab, Wyatt? I feel like I owe you something."

"No . . . no thank you."

"Take some. I've even got some pies made up ready for cooking. Be happy to give you a dozen."

Wyatt grinned ruefully. "Jim, I've eaten a lot of things in my life, but somehow I just can't bring myself to eat uncleaned half-growed pigeons that are still wearing their feet."

The man called James Y. Johnson laughed easily. "Tell you the truth, Wyatt," he declared as he rose to his feet, "I don't blame you. I don't eat them either. I just throw out three tons of wheat a day, gather the pigeons in, take their babies, pop their necks, and ship them out. Then I smile all the way to the bank."

Both men laughed heartily, shook hands, and then together walked out into the increasingly intense October storm. And, at least from this visit, Wyatt Earp carried no further ghosts.

Chapter 18

When Ruby opened her door in response to the insistent knocking, she was shocked at the coolness of the air. For over a week the days had been glorious and warm. But now, with almost no warning at all, the temperatures had lowered so far that the men outside were wearing overcoats and their breath swirled away in frosty mist.

"H-hello, Marshal," she said, her voice catching in her throat.

"Mornin', Mrs. Alder. It's turned off mighty cold out here, hasn't it."

Silently Ruby nodded. She was frightened by the cold, but not for her. She was frightened for Johnny. What on earth would he do? He had no coat, no warm home to stay in . . .

"May we come in?" Marshal Hamilton asked.

"Of . . . of course."

The three men entered the warmth of Ruby's home, and she bade them be seated.

"Mrs. Alder," Marshal Hamilton said, "this is Marshal Bill Bromley, and of course you know George Cunningham, American Fork's city justice."

"How do you do, gentlemen."

"Mrs. Alder, we . . . uh . . . we have a warrant for the arrest of John Phips. If he's here, we'd like you to get him for us."

"A . . . a warrant? But on what charge?"

"Arson, Mrs. Alder. Arson and attempted murder."

Ruby's ears pounded with the sudden pressure that filled her head, and for a moment she thought she was going to faint. He hadn't done those things—she *knew* he hadn't! Why couldn't they see it? Why on earth did Willy—

"Did Willy sign the . . . the warrant?"

"The complaint, ma'am. He signed the complaint, and the judge issued the warrant. Is Mr. Phips here?"

"No . . . no he isn't."

"We have a search warrant as well, ma'am. In case it should appear that you are harboring him."

Suddenly Ruby was angry, and it showed in her eyes. "Are you questioning my integrity, Marshal Hamilton?"

"Well, ma'am, it is known that you are not a disinterested party. Mr. Alder, your son, told us to expect little cooperation from you; and so we came prepared for whatever we might find."

"Willy told you *that?*"

"Yes, ma'am. He did."

"That surprises me," Ruby mused. "I thought he knew me better . . . Gentlemen, my home is yours. Look as you will."

"It is known that he lodged in your barn, ma'am."

"Oh, by all means look there as well. In fact, look in the privy, the garage, the outbuildings; look where you will. I have told you that he's not here, and he isn't. I haven't seen him since the explosion last night."

"Thank you, Mrs. Alder. We'll take our look around and then be on our way."

Ruby nodded anxiously, the men began their search, and with hammering heart she sat in her parlor worrying. Where was Johnny Phips? It was getting terribly cold outside, the law was after him for charges that her own son had filed, and she was scared.

So far as she knew, Johnny didn't even have an overcoat. But maybe he wouldn't need one. Maybe he had caught a train and had gone out of town in the same manner he had come in. Perhaps even now he was nearing Los Angeles . . .

No! He wouldn't do that! He wouldn't leave without telling her that he was going. Johnny surely must know how she felt about him. He was a good man, likely even the best man she had ever known. Surely he wouldn't do such a thing to her. To think that was to deny—

"Ma'am?"

"Yes?" she started, turning to face the men.

"There's nothing here, ma'am. We're sorry to have troubled you, and we'll be on our way."

"Thank you."

"You're welcome. And ma'am, if you should happen to see him, we would appreciate a call."

"No, Marshal Hamilton," Ruby declared emphatically, "I won't call. To tell you I would, would be a lie, and I don't lie! John Phips is innocent, and I know it. If you and my well-meaning son would just listen to a few things, you'd know it too."

"Mrs. Alder," Marshal Hamilton said quietly, "with this warrant, it has gone some beyond my listening. You can tell me all you want, and it won't do either one of us any good. Now the issue is for a judge to decide. Please remember that, and remember all that you know, too. We'll catch the old man, and when we do, you will very likely be called upon to testify."

"What if Willy were to drop his complaint?"

"That'd change things some. Our office would still want to talk with John Phips, but only to question him. The only charge we might have would be a 'suspicion' charge."

Ruby sighed. "Very well. Thank you for coming."

"Thank you, ma'am. Have a nice day."

The three men walked out into the cold, and Ruby stood silently, watching them go. She felt so helpless, so old and foolish and inept. Where could Johnny have gone, and how could she possibly help him now that he had?

Turning away from the door, Ruby was startled to see a boy straining his bicycle up the hill, fighting the wind as he strove toward her house. Quickly she stepped out into the cold to see what he wanted.

"M-Mrs. Alder," he gasped as he reached her gate, "telegram here for you."

"Telegram?" Ruby echoed in surprise.

"Yes'm. Here it is."

"Do I owe you anything? I mean, I've never received a telegram before, and—"

"No, ma'am," the youth declared as he beat his hands together to get them warm again. "Not, that is, unless you want to."

Ruby smiled warmly. "Well, come inside then, and be quick about it."

The boy followed, and Ruby opened her purse and took out a silver dollar.

"Is this enough?"

The boy's mouth hung open for an instant, and then quickly he gulped and nodded. "Yes, ma'am, enough and a whole lot more besides. I only make two bits a day, so I don't think you ought to give me all this."

"Oh, stuff and nonsense!" Ruby declared sternly. "Take it and be gone with you."

The youth thanked her, took the dollar, and sprinted for his bike, his mind no doubt filled with visions of where he would invest his newly acquired wealth.

Ruby watched him go, closed the door, and looked at the telegram. Finally, with heart pounding, she tore it open, very carefully, and then she read:

JAKE STOP W EARP SAYS MCNAMARAS OLD ED PLATT HOME PLEASANT GROVE STOP LOCUST STREET FACES MOUNTAINS ROCK STOP BE CAREFUL STOP LOVE TO FAMILY STOP JAMES Y. JOHNSON

Ruby read the cursory telegram over and over. She was certain that she knew what it meant, but how would it help now? Jake had to be Johnny, for the man on the telephone a day or so before had used that name. That also meant that the McNamaras were located in Pleasant Grove. Only how could *she* capture them? How could this telegram from her younger brother possibly do any good? What could she possibly do?

No, not her, she realized. How could *Johnny* do anything about it? He was nowhere to be found. Or was he? Might he even now be out in the barn? Could he have sneaked in and hidden from the marshals?

Quickly taking up her shawl, Ruby hurried out the back door and ran to the barn.

"Johnny!" she called. "Johnny Phips, are you in here?"

There was no answer save for the wind and the soft lowing of her old milk cow.

"Johnny, if you are here, make yourself known to me this instant! I have news, and it's terribly important!"

She waited, her breath stilled in anticipation, her eyes peering into every corner of the old barn. "Johnny—"

"He ain't here, ma'am."

In surprise Ruby spun to face the sober-faced marshal she had met earlier. He held a rifle in his hand, and she could see that he was very serious.

"What . . . what are *you* doing here?"

"Guarding you, Mrs. Alder. That man's dangerous, and there's no telling what he might do to you if he should return. Now about that terribly important news you wanted to tell him . . ."

"It . . . it was nothing," Ruby stammered. "I wanted him to know that you folks were after him."

"And the telegram?"

"It was from my brother."

"May I see it?"

"I . . . I . . ."

"Ma'am."

Slowly Ruby handed the yellow document to the marshal, who scanned it quickly.

"Who's Jake?"

"It . . . it's a name he made up."

The marshal grinned. "Yeah, I call my sister Fred, too. I made it up when we were just kids. She doesn't mind, but no one else would understand. And who is W. Earp? The famous Wyatt, no doubt?"

And with that the marshal laughed with genuine mirth, almost doubling over at such a ludicrous thought.

"And the McNamaras?" he gasped, trying to be serious again.

"People he . . . he wants me to look up."

"He says to be careful. Must be boorish relatives, huh."

"I . . . I guess that's as good a way to put it as any. I'm sure that's why he told me to be careful."

"I know folks like that, myself—I'm related to more than a few of 'em. When you see 'em coming, you want to lock the door and go hide in the root cellar. These McNamara folks just get into town, did they?"

"I think last week."

"Well, Mrs. Alder, I wish you luck with 'em. And don't you worry none about this Phips fellow. We'll get him."

The deputy lifted his rifle and patted it. Ruby did her best to smile, and then she took the telegram and walked back to her home.

For a moment she stood inside the closed door, shivering and thinking. She was being guarded, not protected, and no matter what the marshal out there said, she knew the truth. Willy didn't trust her, and neither did any of the others. Nor, for a fact, did she blame them.

Slowly Ruby turned and walked back into her parlor, where she sat and took up the old teakwood box that contained the treasures of her youth. Slowly she went through them, letting her memories carry her into times past when things had seemed happier, sadder, easier, and more difficult.

Life, she thought ruefully, never seemed to change much. It was one long series of terrible crises, with lulls between them that were composed only of more crises that didn't seem so terrible. It was no wonder that the Lord had instructed his children to *'endure* to the end.' He surely hadn't said 'skip' or 'slide' or 'walk easily.' Life was an endurance test, pure and simple.

And while enduring, what was she going to do about John Phips? What *should* she do?

"Dear God in heaven," she prayed in desperation, "I've got troubles, real troubles, and I don't know where to turn. Johnny is innocent, I feel that he is, I know he . . .

"Lord, *is* Johnny innocent?"

Ruby waited then, as she had learned through her life to wait, exercising her faith by telling the Lord that she knew he could give her an answer, and that she wasn't budging until it came.

And so it did, a warm sweet feeling that filled her heart and mind with the peaceful understanding that Johnny *was* innocent.

"Thank you, Lord," she whispered, "for that answer. Now I have one more question. Will you protect him from my son Willy and those well-thinking men of the law who are seeking him?"

Again she paused to wait, and almost instantly the certainty was there again, a confirmation that John Phips would indeed be protected.

But being a practical woman, Ruby understood that the Lord usually performed his miracles through his children. Only who on earth could possibly . . .

In silence she stared at a photo in her lap, a very old photo of a young man seated with a young woman standing behind him. It was an often-looked-at-photo, yellowed with age, and with two names at the bottom. A man and a woman, stern-faced as in all old photographs, but obviously in love.

So, she thought, men and women frequently fell in love. And when they did, what was a woman's responsibility to that man? Especially what was her responsibility when the man that she loved had such troubles as John Phips was having?

And she loved John Phips—she knew that she did. Willy was right; it didn't make much sense. But it was true, and there was nothing she could do about it.

Now John Phips, the man she loved more than life itself, was in trouble, serious trouble. And *she* was the only one left who might be able to help him. But how *could* she help? Just how did a seventy-year-old, formerly polygamous widow go about finding a chance of survival for a seventy-two-year-old fugitive from justice, even a slim chance? Where could she turn? Who could she ask for help?

Not her family, for that was too much to expect. Not the Church, for the same reason. And not the law; that was out as well.

So if she could get no help in preventing a terrible miscarriage of justice, whom could she turn to?

The answer was obvious, and hopeless.

There was only Ruby Soderberg Alder left to help the lonely old man through his ordeal.

And who was there to help her?

Nobody. Not a solitary mortal soul.

Or was there?

Other than Johnny, she had but two people she felt she might trust in this situation. The first was her granddaughter, Allyson Alder, who might just as quickly go to her father as not. And she should, Ruby decided instantly. A young girl should never be torn away from her father. So Allyson was out.

And that left only the highly unusual and outspoken Ferdinand Burroughs, who acted as quirky when he had no reason to, as ever he did when he was in public. And who was just as likely to be spouting poetry in Latin or complaining about his irrascible family as he was to be listening to and helping Ruby Alder with her problems.

Still, the beset woman's mind grounded on the thought of that tall, scrawny, dour, pimple-faced youngster. For all his eccentricities and outlandish stories, Ferd was a good boy, and smart. If anybody could help her, he just might be the one.

White-faced, growing sicker inside with every passing minute, Ruby Alder closed her box of memories and stood. Then with measured step she walked to the wooden telephone on the wall.

"Effie," she shouted after she had rung through to central, "I want to talk to the Burroughs home—Ferdinand Burroughs. And Effie, this is a *private* conversation! Thank you."

Chapter 19

"Hello, Flora," Ruby said as she stood on the front porch of her son's home, shivering with cold. "Is Willy at home?"

"He is," Flora responded with a smile. "Come in out of the cold, Mother. Isn't that open automobile a terrible cold thing to drive in weather like this?"

"It is, and I will come in. It surely feels like a storm is coming."

"Hard to believe, after the weather we've been having. Sit down, and I'll get Will for you."

"Hi, Grandma."

"Hello, Allyson. How are you today?"

"Well, to tell the truth, I'm scared. Grandma, how could that nice old man try to murder Daddy?"

"He didn't, Allyson. You were with us all day, so you ought to know—"

"Grandma, I saw him leave the dance last night. He was gone a long time, too."

"Yes, he left, but not to . . . to bomb your father's office."

"But how do you *know* that?"

"Allyson, you know John Phips quite well now. Except for me and Ferdinand, you've spent more time with him than anybody else. Knowing of him like you do, do you think Johnny could ever do such a terrible thing?"

"Grandma, I don't know how to tell. I wouldn't have thought so, but Daddy says—"

"I say what?" William Alder asked as he strode into the room. "I say what, Allyson?"

"You . . . you say that John Phips's guilt is a lead-pipe cinch."

"That's true. It is. That thief's guilt has been written all over his face since the day he marched into town and maliciously swept Mother off her feet. I've warned you, too, haven't I, Mother."

"Yes, Willy, you warned me. Only—"

"Just Monday last, at the dedication, I confronted him and confounded him in his guilt. And oh, he took it hard, he did. Mumbled and stumbled and finally ended up threatening me in that silly speech. And he made a try, too, with that bomb. It's just a lucky thing I forgot and left my light on last night, making it look like I was there. Otherwise the old fool might have tried my home."

"Willy, please don't. You don't understand."

"I understand that he's gone," William declared, interrupting her. "I can't say that I'm sorry, except I do wish they could have apprehended him quickly. Now it appears that it will take a little longer."

"They're not going to catch him, Willy. He's innocent, and the Lord has promised me that Johnny will be protected."

"Innocent!" William stormed. "Good heavens, Mother, what is it going to *take?* First he comes into town and takes advantage of you—"

"Willy, that is a lie, and I won't stand for you speaking of him like that. You know better, for I have told you!"

"A lie? Come, Mother—"

"Very well, I see that you need to receive an accounting. In clothing and shoes, I gave John Phips, my hired hand, thirty-two dollars, none of which he asked for. In food, I imagine that I've spent no more that ten dollars more than I would have spent feeding just myself. In actual cash wages, I have not paid him one single dollar.

"Now Willy, suppose that Sister Trimble down here came to you and asked you to dig her potatoes. What would you do?"

"I'd assign her block teachers or the Aaronic priesthood—"

"No, Willy, you misunderstood. I mean you personally. How much would you charge her to dig her potatoes?"

"Mother, she couldn't afford me. My time is worth too much."

"Yes, you are probably right. It's also too valuable to spend on your mother. So who is there to dig my potatoes, or paint my fence or the trim on my home? Who is there, Willy, to chop my winter fire-wood? Who is there to repair the barn and the fences, to mend the well, to stop the erosion behind the barn, to sharpen the ax, to brand the calf, to milk the cow morning and night—"

"Mother, except for the milking, I will get at all those things."

"Yes, Willy, I know. In eternity, or after you are released from being bishop; and after you stop being famous, which I think is probably the same thing."

"Now, that isn't fair!"

"Maybe not, but it is true. Willy, John Phips, in this one short week, has accomplished every single one of these tasks that I have listed. You no longer need to worry about them. How much, in dollars and cents, would that week be worth to you?"

William stood silently, his mind unable to stop adding up the hours such a work-week might cost him. Ruby could see that she had him thinking, so rather than give him the opportunity to think of a lower figure, she continued.

"The answer, Willy, is considerably more than forty-two dollars, and you know it. Especially if you were to pay yourself to do the work. Now pay attention to your mother. *Never again will you accuse Mr. John Phips of taking advantage of a poor, defenseless widow-woman.* Do you hear me?"

William sighed. "Yes, Mother, I hear you. Now tell me how I can use that same illogical formula for deciding that the old man did me a favor when he bombed my office and tried to kill me."

"He didn't do it, Willy."

"Oh, Mother, he did so! All the evidence points to it. Other than that detective fellow who was looking for him, he's been the only stranger in town."

"But Willy—"

"Mother, with what we know of his past, and with his presence here verified, the circumstantial evidence is overwhelming. That old man bombed my office. What's more, he tried to kill me in it. That you are still defending the man who tried to murder your only son is so overwhelming to me that I cannot comprehend it.

"Mother, let me tell you a little about him. The Molly Maguires were a secret society, akin to the Gadianton Robbers in the Book of

Mormon, who robbed and murdered to get gain and to achieve their own selfish political labor goals. They had legitimate gripes, but they chose illegal means to achieve them. John Phips was a Molly Maguire."

"You don't know that."

"But I do. He was there the week they were wiped out, way back in 1877. It's a wonder that he wasn't hanged with the rest of them. Since then, every time a subversive labor group has surfaced in our country, your man has been there, right in the middle of that group. He was even in Los Angeles three weeks ago when Harrison Gray Otis's newspaper office was bombed. Of course you already know he was there, for that ne'er-do-well brother of yours sent him from there to here. Or at least so Phips claims.

"Mother, the *Times* is a powerful voice against organized labor. When Phips bombed it on October first, twenty people were killed. Did you hear that, Mother? Twenty!

"John Phips is a rabid animal who kills indiscriminately. He tried to kill me, and I will not rest until he is apprehended and brought to justice."

"Willy, I know that all you say is historically accurate, all except for Johnny. He didn't do those things. He couldn't! And especially he couldn't attempt to murder you. The Lord told me that he is innocent, and I know he is. With all my heart I feel it."

"Mother, you don't *know* he's innocent. You're responding emotionally, and emotions always cloud issues."

"Then why did the Lord give us emotions, Willy?"

"I don't know, Mother. I just—"

Ruby smiled. "There! *You don't know*. How thrilled I am to hear you admit that you still remember those words. You don't know. Isn't that a wonderful phrase, Willy? Even the Founding Fathers used it, and governed their writing of the Constitution by it."

"What?"

"Willy, none of us *know*, except as things are manifest to us by the power of the Spirit. You may be a bishop and therefore a judge in Israel, but you are not John Phips's bishop. Therefore, you have no right to be his judge and jury, nor will the Holy Ghost have informed you of his guilt. Therefore, until such time as a *legally* assigned judge and jury of his peers hear his case, *if* that is ever necessary, John Phips has the right to be presumed innocent. I grant him that right and would hope that the renowned Will Alder, champion of the rights of free men throughout the nation, would also grant it."

William Alder stood silently, and Ruby could see that he was wrestling mentally with her logic, trying to find a hole through which he could reach to turn it around. *You poor boy,* she thought. *Don't you know that you had to get your great gift for logic from somewhere? I may not be as skilled, but put my back to the wall, and you've got a real argument ahead of you, son. A real one.*

"Mother," William finally said, "all that you have postulated is true, and I have no argument with it. What I don't understand is this: There is, legitimately and legally, suspicion directed against the man in connection with the bombing of *my* office. That being the case, how can you so actively take his case as opposed to mine?"

Ruby took a deep breath, then sighed. "Are you sure that you want to know?"

"I do."

"Very well, sit down and I will tell you. I had hoped that if it ever came to this, that Johnny would be with me. But . . . It is a long story, Willy, and you must promise to be still until I finish—"

Ruby was interrupted by a loud knocking upon William Alder's front door. All waited, and seconds later Allyson spoke from the hallway.

"Daddy, it's the marshal."

William excused himself and strode into the foyer of his home, and Ruby, almost unconsciously, arose and followed.

"Yes, Harvey?"

"Will, we've got a lead. Someone saw a feller up the canyon, near Tibble Fork. Said it looked a lot like our man."

"Tibble Fork, huh. Now how would he know about the canyon, I wonder?"

"Daddy, I . . . I . . ."

"Yes, Allyson?"

Allyson turned nervously, looking at her father and then at Ruby. "I . . . uh . . ."

"Tell him, Allyson," Ruby said quietly. "He ought to know."

Allyson smiled thankfully at her grandmother and then hurriedly spoke to her father.

"Daddy, Grandma told Ferd and me that she rode up there with Johnny Phips last Sunday, showing him the sights."

William looked at his daughter, and then he turned to Ruby, who was still standing by the door to the parlor.

"Mother, is that true?"

"It is."

"Well, men, that's it. Let's get a posse together and get moving."

"But Willy, I wanted to tell you—"

"No, Mother, not now. There'll be plenty of time to talk when John Phips is behind bars."

"Willy, the day will come when you'll be sorry—"

But William cut her off, laughing. "Sorry, Mother? Sorry to be *alive?* The only thing I am sorry about is that I waited so long to get the law after him. Now, have Flora fix you some warm broth, and we'll continue our little talk when I return."

With that he took his overcoat and was gone. And Ruby, Flora, and Allyson stood silently in the cold of the open doorway, watching the men depart.

"I'm sorry, Mother," Flora declared gently. "I do wish that there was an easier way."

"I . . . I'm sorry, too," Allyson said as sudden tears streamed down her face. "Grandma, I feel so torn! I like Johnny, I love you, and I love Daddy. Was I wrong in telling him? What . . . what am I supposed to do?"

Ruby took the girl in her arms. "You did just right, sweetheart. A girl should always support her father. And Flora, you should always support your husband. That's the right thing to do. I can't even blame Willy for thinking as he does."

"But . . . but I *feel* so guilty," Allyson declared.

"Well, you shouldn't. You couldn't help it, either of you, for you simply don't understand. I'm not even certain that *I* understand everything. But one of these days, when things all come to light, please don't feel too badly about this, either of you."

"What? But Grandma, I don't know what you mean."

"I don't understand, either, Mother. Are you really certain of John Phips's innocence?"

"Positive. I know him, and I know he has been trying all week to protect my family, especially Willy. That's why he had you stand out in your yard on Monday. I think he was trying to frighten the men who did the bombing."

"But how would that frighten them?" Flora asked.

"I'm not certain, but at least they wouldn't dare come into your yard in open daylight and put a bomb under your home. If no one had been visible, they might have done just that."

"Yes," Flora agreed thoughtfully. "I see. I . . . But Mother, who *is* he, and why would he be trying to protect our family?"

"I . . . I can't tell you, Flora. I'm sorry. Willy should be told first, and then if he wishes—"

"Grandma, I really want to believe that Johnny is innocent. I really do."

"Of course you do. And you will, Allyson. I promise. *All* of my family will believe. Now I really must run. Good-bye, my darlings. I love both of you more than I can ever say."

"We love you too, Mother."

Ruby smiled. "I know. That's why I have the courage to go ahead. Bye."

"Bye, Grandma."

Ruby wrapped her shawl about her neck and walked outside to her automobile. There she set the magneto, cranked the car until it started, and then wearily climbed in.

So now the law knew about the canyon, she thought as she pulled out into the road. They knew, Ferdinand had not come back, and so there was only one thing left to do.

Pray.

Chapter 20

"Hi, G-Grandma Alder."

The wind was blowing terribly, there was a touch of sleet in the air, and Ruby Alder was cold. She was also relieved that Ferdinand had returned, and she could see that he was cold, too. Yet she was not through with the young man, not quite. He still had at least one more mission, though even he didn't know of it. But he was a smart boy; and she hoped, with the right questions, to inspire him to give the *right* answers.

She also hoped to keep him out on the porch for a moment or so longer, and so she purposely stood with the door partly closed, blocking his way.

"Ferdinand," she shouted so that her voice would carry above the wind, "what a nice surprise. You look terribly cold."

"I am!" Ferdinand shouted back. "It's freezing up that canyon, and it's even starting to snow."

"Up the canyon?" Ruby questioned in mock surprise, keeping the shivering and slightly confused Ferdinand on the porch. "What on earth were you doing up there?"

For an instant Ferdinand looked at her, his face registering his surprise. But Ruby flicked her eyes back and forth from the corner of the house, and suddenly Ferdinand grinned.

"Why was I up the canyon? Why, ma'am, that's a powerful long story. My Pa's Aunt Frieda and her husband, Long Tom Plunket, had a few cows up there, and Aunt Frieda she says to Long Tom—"

"Did you find them up there?" Ruby shouted.

"No, ma'am, I did not! Pa'll be mighty worried, too, for he was fixin' on gettin' one of their cows for our winter beef, and—"

"Did you see anybody else up there, Ferdinand?"

Again Ferdinand paused, confused. But Ruby nodded encouragingly, and the youth, understanding at least partly, slowly answered.

"Yes, yes I did."

"Oh, my goodness. Who on earth would be up there on a day like this?"

Again Ruby got a questioning look, and again she encouraged the young man to answer.

"Well," he said slowly, so that she could shut him off should he say something he shouldn't, "I met a feller up there, name of . . . of John Phips."

"John Phips!" Ruby shouted. "You mean the man who stayed out in my barn? Why, I thought he'd gone."

With that Ruby winked and lifted her hands slightly, as though she were a choir director encouraging her group to greater volume. Ferdinand understood perfectly and launched quite loudly into one of his 'accounts'.

"It was John Phips, all right! He was fixin' to leave, too. Up over the top, he said. Minds me of the time that Pa's uncle's wife's brother, fellow by the name of Zeus Taylor, tried to cross up there with a storm comin' in on him. Pa's uncle, he tried to warn Zeus out of it, but Zeus was a stubborn man, he was, and wouldn't talk out of it for nothing. Says he, 'I'm a'goin', and I'm a'goin' alone,' he says. And he went, too. Guess he figured since he was named after one of them Greek god fellers, he'd have extry power or something. Did pretty good, I'm told, though no one knew it till the next spring, when he was found about halfway down into Heber Valley, curled up under some mighty thin bushes, and deader'n last fall's leaves. I tried to tell ol' Phips that, but he was determined, and last I saw of him he was headin' up Tibble Fork like the devil hisself was on his trail. But it's snowing up there, ma'am, and I do worry. Fact is, I think maybe I ought to report it to the marshal."

"I agree, Ferdinand. Why don't you come in and use my telephone?"

Ruby smiled, Ferdinand entered, and seconds later they both heard the rapidly departing sound of hooves as the marshal headed for the canyon.

"Who's that?" Ferdinand asked as Ruby poured the shivering youth a cup of hot postum.

"One of our marshals. That was wonderful, Ferdinand. You did that just right."

"Well, ma'am, it was about the truth, if you know what I mean."

"Wh-what?"

"I found Johnny, ma'am, and he was fixin' to do exactly as I said outside. He told me he was beat and couldn't see any possible way out of it. Howsomever, I told him you had an urgent message to give him that might color his decision somewhat, and so he reconsidered. He was waverin' considerable anyway, what with thinkin' of you, but word of that there message turned him total. If he can work his way past that posse sweeping up the canyon, he'll be back to see you."

"If he doesn't get past them, well . . ."

"Ferdinand," Ruby declared as she took the boy's empty cup, "you've no idea how much I appreciate what you've done. I know that weather is miserable, and I know you've had quite a ride."

"Yes, ma'am, it was. Minds me of the time—"

"Ferd?"

Ferdinand Burroughs grinned. "All right, Grandma Alder. I'll close my yap. And I'll be home in case you and . . . well, in case you should need me again. And please call. Another couple of adventures like this and I won't never have to talk about my goofy relatives again. I can spend my days bragging upon myownself."

Ruby smiled, hugged the young man, and saw him to the door. Then, with her teakwood box in her lap, she sat and began once again to wait.

Chapter 21

The Regulator clock showed just after three in the afternoon when Ruby came suddenly awake. She had no idea what had awakened her, but the room was chilly, and so stiffly she rose to her feet to stoke the fire.

To her chagrin, however, the woodbox was empty. And so with a sigh Ruby took her shawl and walked outside to go to the woodpile. But on the porch she paused, almost reluctant to move into the face of the growing storm.

Tightening the shawl, however, she stepped to the edge of the porch and—

"Top of the afternoon to ye, Ruby lass. And what might ye be wantin' to fetch out here in this haythun storm? Faith, now, and the blessed mercury has dived so far down in the bulb that ye can't see it with a spyglass."

With a gasp of surprise, Ruby looked down to see the wrinkled, tired face of John Phips smiling up at her from the wash-bench upon which he was seated.

"J-Johnny?"

"At yer sarvice, me ravishin' beauty. Mercy, me lass, I take sober oath that yer gettin' purtier ev'ry garjus day of yer life!"

"Johnny, look at you! Just sitting in this storm, and without a coat, too. Get in the house this second, before you catch your death of cold!"

"Ah, it's a temper, is it? Faith, but I thought ye'd grown out of that weakness in yer soul—"

"Weakness? Listen, you fake Irish hypocrite . . ."

Johnny coughed. "Now there's the Ruby I've fallen in love with. You want wood, do you? Well, while you slept the sleep of the innocent, I've stacked your porch here with it. And if that isn't enough, I'll stack more until you won't be able to get out the door."

Standing slowly, John reached down and took up a few sticks of wood. Then, with a lopsided grin and a painful-looking limp, he followed Ruby into her cozy kitchen. There he proceeded to stoke up her stove.

"Well," he said when the fire was blazing and he had a hot drink in his hand, "the lad said you had urgent news."

"Sit down and drink your drink, and I'll tell you when you are finished. Good news can always wait, and bad news ought to."

Nodding, Johnny sat in the old horsehair rocker with his drink, and Ruby walked to her place of refuge at the sink, where she busied herself cleaning that which had already been cleaned.

Oh, her heart cried, *what are you going to do with this sick and tired old man called John Phips? It is hardly a trick at all, when he is away and out of sight, to shudder and tell yourself that he has no place in your life. Or even to see the way he looks at you, like no man has looked in more years than you care to remember, and be afraid of him. It is easy to say, when you have listened to your good and only son describe this man, that he is a deceiver and that you never want to see him again in your soft little life. It is easy to believe that he is a liar and a man who gives hurt, and that what is between the two of you isn't, nor ever was. It is easy, that is, when he is off and far away.*

But when he is sitting across a two-foot table from you in the toasty-warm lamplight of your cozy home, with nothing between you and the exciting look of him but fifty-some years of waiting and the low arm of an old horsehair rocker, it is quite another, confusingly passionate, matter.

Still, Ruby Soderberg Alder, where you don't know yourself, and where you certainly don't know the strange old man with the soft blue eyes and the easy, flattering tongue who is beguiling you, you do know right from wrong. John Phips, innocent or guilty, is a man wanted by the authorities in your beloved state of Utah. No decent woman, knowing what you know of his whereabouts, could move

*another mortal step with him along the unknown path he wills you to
follow.*

*Only you love him! You poor, miserable fool, with all your heart
you love him, and you know you will do all that he says—*

"Well?" he asked quietly.

Without a word Ruby handed him the telegram, and then she
stood trembling only slightly while he slowly read it.

"Ahhh," he breathed, "Imagine that! James and the famous
Wyatt Earp. I'll bet those two had a lot to talk about."

"Johnny, the telegram!"

John grinned, coughing again as he spoke. "Yes, this could be
important. I *knew* they were in Pleasant Grove. Even when we lost
them, I felt it in my bones. The question is, are they still there now?"

"I . . . I don't know."

"I imagine the only way to find out is to go and see. Have you
heard from Frank Burns?"

Ruby shook her head.

"Neither have I. But I don't think he'd leave town without getting word to me, so that means he must still be around."

"Do you know where he was staying, Johnny?"

"Yes. Down at the Grant Hotel. Would you mind ringing him up
on the telephone for me?"

Without answering, Ruby walked to the telephone and rang central. "Effie," she called, "ring me the Grant Hotel. What? The storm?
Very well. I said, *ring . . . me . . . the . . . Grant . . . Hotel!* Did
you hear me? Good."

For a moment there was silence, and then Ruby shouted again,
asking for the guest named Frank Burns.

"What?" she called. "When? Very well. When he returns—
What? Oh . . . I . . . see! Then . . . give . . . him . . . this . . .
message . . ."

And loudly and slowly, Ruby gave the information she had ob-
tained from the telegram.

"Now what do we do?" she asked when she had rung off.

"I suppose *we* just stay put. *I* will go—"

"Oh no you don't, Mr. Phips. From now on, where you go, I go.
That's final!"

"You really feel that way, Ruby?"

"I . . . I do."

John smiled. "Thank you, darling. So do I."

"You . . . you do?"

"I do. Up that canyon, thinking about going over the top and leaving you, I did a little thinking of my own. I decided, up there in the wind and the cold, that a person has to face up to himself sometime or other. You can go on being satisfied or ducking the issue only so long, and then there comes a time when you start asking yourself, not what you've done with your summer's wages, but with your whole life's earnings up to that point.

"The thing we have to realize is that it's never too late. I've known many people who have braced up and made something of themselves after they were forty or fifty or sixty, with nothing to show for the years before that but scars and the cluttering up of dead wishes. I don't know if it will work at seventy, but I'd like to give it a try.

"About the worst thing a person can do, Ruby, is to let a dream die. Long ago, when I wasn't much more than a youngster, I used to dream of having my own place, and of just how I'd handle it. I even found a girl, the perfect girl, and made her a part of my dream. Ruby, an idea like that, a dream, doesn't just lie fallow; it builds up and gathers background, trying to fit itself for realization. Even if nothing seems to happen, yet it does. Here and there you pick up an idea or a thought, you work for somebody else who does well or badly, you see a lot of different women and you compare them with the perfect one you've found, and thus you add to your little stock of information. And you do it mostly without thinking.

"You get to studying things out, thinking deeply, trying to understand why things didn't work out like you thought and even hoped they would. Every idea you have about that is like a seed; and like a seed, it germinates. Only you have to feed it and make it grow properly.

"You were surprised the other day when I told you that I had read Elder Whitney's works? Well, that's why I read them. I was feeding my ideas and understanding. My trouble was that after a lot of years of thinking, I'd sort of fallen into the rut of taking things as they came and moving on if I didn't like them. My idea of a place and family of my own was still there, I imagine, but it was mighty spindly, and growing weaker by the year.

"Ruby, people never get old until they start to forget their dreams. I've started growing old. Somebody once said that nature abhors a vacuum. Well, from all I've seen, I'd say that God abhors anything that doesn't produce. And me? Well, up in that canyon I decided that if I was going to give up one more time on that dream of a place of my own and that perfect woman to go with it, especially now that I knew where that perfect woman was, well, I'd ought to just give up and die instead.

"But Ruby, darling, I can't. My dream isn't dead. Until a few days ago it had been lying there, starving for lack of hope. But then your brother sent me flyin' this way, I saw you on that back porch, and suddenly it was alive and well. If you'll have me, I'll spend whatever amounts to the rest of my life, doing my best to protect you and to make you happy."

"Oh, Johnny . . ." Ruby sighed, her eyes moist with love and . . . and the belonging she had so long sought for. And she knew at that moment, with that certain knowledge that is occasionally planted in the hearts of women, that no matter what happened, no matter what turned out to be his history, she would stand beside John Phips forever. And she would do so happily, with no regrets.

Only, and she hated herself for thinking this, could she really believe what he was saying?

"Now don't you say a thing," Johnny was saying. "You think about it, and if we can lay our hands on those McNamara boys and get them shipped back to Los Angeles with Frank, then you can tell me."

"But I already know—"

John stopped her with his hand on her lips. "Not now. Do you think Ferdinand can help us again?"

Ruby nodded and rang him up, and shortly the three, bundled heavily, were sliding and spinning through the icy mud toward Pleasant Grove, Utah.

Chapter 22

The capture of the McNamara brothers, when it came, was surprisingly easy. Because John was known to the two, he and Ruby hid behind some outbuildings and sent Ferdinand to the front door.

Loudly he knocked, again and again. Ruby had almost decided that they had missed the murderers when suddenly the door opened and a dark-visaged man stood there.

"Good afternoon," Ferdinand declared joyfully. "Sir, my name is Ferdinand Burroughs, Ferd for short, and I am earning my way through school selling the handiest little kitchen gadget you have ever seen in your life. It is good for peeling fruit—"

"Not interested," the man growled as he started to shut the door.

"Not interested? But sir, you have no idea—"

"I said—"

"Yes, but did you know that this wonderful little tool will unlock even the most puzzling lock? It will, I tell you. It will even decode the combination of the strongest safe, so in case you lock yourself out of a safe, you can take this little tool—"

"It'll unlock safes?" the man asked, his interest sparked.

"Oh, my goodness, yes! The Jiffy Kitchen Joy Tool—that's what it's called, by the way—will even crack bank safes, though of course you wouldn't be interested in that. But I have a cousin, Bartholomew James, he is called, direct descendant of the notorious Jesse James, I believe he is, who this very month told me, he says, 'Ferd, I'm a wealthy man,' he says. I say, 'Wealthy? But Bart, last I heard you was poor as a church mouse.' And he says, 'I was, but you sold me that handy little Jiffy Kitchen Joy Tool,' he says, 'and now some banks will be somewhat poorer but I'll never have need of money again', he says. Mister, I was some startled, for of course you've read of the same string of bank robberies that I've read of, and speaking of robberies, Pa's aunt Pernicious Humdrum bought one of these little Jiffy Kitchen Joy Tools, and let me tell you, she turned herself into a whiz at perpetratin' the most gosh-awful home burglaries . . ."

Ferd went on, while the poor man who listened was made a slack-jawed captive in his own doorway.

"Ruby," John whispered as he led her around to the back door, "I swear, that kid'll out-talk the bishop at his own funeral. I think he'll die of old age long before ever he runs down!"

Ruby only had time to smile before John pushed her against the side of the rock house and told her to stay put. Then, producing a small revolver from somewhere inside his coat, he quietly opened the door and passed inside.

Little more than a minute or so later he reappeared, two hand-cuffed brothers grumbling before his unwavering pistol. He was thanking Ferdinand for his help when a team loomed out of the gathering twilight, and the man Ruby had seen several times before jumped down and hurried toward them.

"Good work, Johnny," the man called Frank Burns declared as he gazed at the men in cuffs. "I'd have thought they'd be gone."

"We would have," the obviously older of the two snarled, "if this idiot hadn't met some handsome little fillie at that church meeting we went to the other day. 'One more night,' he says. 'One more night . . .'"

"Aw, that wasn't nothin'," the younger one growled. "You was the one got suckered into that Jiffy Kitchen Joy Tool setup!"

"So'd you, you lummox! You was standin' right behind me with both your big ears bugled out, takin' that safe-crackin' nonsense right in. Besides, did you have a listen at this kid? I ain't never met a man with so much axle-grease on the hinges of his jawbones. Kid, where'd you learn to throw verbal lather like that?"

"Well, I . . . that is . . . my pa . . . Say, fellers, speakin' of lather, my pa has a nephew name of Wilbur Peebles that grows facial hair faster'n lizards scoot across hot rocks. And when he shaves, which is about every hour on the hour, why, talk about lather . . ."

Ferdinand continued relating his story to his truly captive audience, and Frank Burns turned to John Phips.

"John, I've got the train holding for us, so we'd best be hurrying. I'll get these fellers loaded while you're saying your goodbyes."

"Frank, put them in the wagon, let Ferd hold the team, and come back for a minute. We need to make a little medicine."

"Are you sure the kid can do that?"

John Phips grinned. "I'll say. Besides a never-stopping mouth, that kid's got more guts than you could stick in a six-hundred-pound steer with a snow shovel. He'll hold 'em good."

"All right, John. I'll be back directly."

Frank Burns did as he was requested, and soon he was back beside the quietly standing couple.

"Well?"

"I won't be going back with you," John said quietly.

"What's that?"

"Frank, I've been waiting all my life to . . . ah . . . to find Ruby here, and now that I finally have, I'm not running off from her, ever."

"Johnny, are you sure?"

"Sure as an old man can be."

"What'll you do about the law?"

"Take you to the police station in American Fork and let you announce that these boys have been arrested for the bombings. Then I figure the heat will be off, and I can tell Ruby's son, William, as well as the local constabulary, the entire story."

"Johnny," Frank Burns said quietly, "I can't do it. Not today, anyway. If I do I'll miss the train, and we'll all be held until tomorrow. That'll completely eliminate the element of surprise, and you know how badly I need that. These birds are only a small part of an illegal scheme that stretches all the way from the northwest, down to the south, and clear back to New York. Before I can make very many announcements to local police, I've got to get after the big boys. Even with this boost, I have at least a year's worth of investigation ahead of me. If I took the time to clear you before I got to Los Angeles, it might jeopardize the whole investigation. Can you hold out until I get back to L.A.?"

John looked down at Ruby. "Can you stand being associated with such a nefarious criminal as myself, even temporarily?"

"I can," Ruby said, gazing admiringly into John's eyes.

"I'll hold out, Frank."

"Good. For a day or so, you'll have to content yourself with being a true, unsung hero. I'm sure you understand."

Quietly Johnny nodded.

"Thanks, Johnny. I'm sorry you must take the brunt of all this."

"Yeah, me, too."

"I'm sorry as well that you won't be with us any longer. John, you're the best that ever was!"

"That's my gift for being average," John said with a smile.

"Well, you're a mighty unique average, old son."

"Thanks. Good luck, Frank."

"Same to you, John. And you too, ma'am. I think you're right, John. She does have the most beautiful of Gibson girl eyes."

Frank winked and then walked silently back to the wagon. "Ferdinand," he said, "could you drive to the station while I keep an eye on these birds? Then you can take the wagon back to the livery. Be happy to pay you, too."

"Be glad to, mister. I've got me a cousin I've been wantin' to elucidate upon, and this seems like a twenty-four carat heaven-sent opportunity. She goes by the name of Abigail Chilene—"

"Mister," the younger of the two anarchists whined, "shut this kid up, will you please?"

"Yeah," the older one agreed heartily. "If he ain't going to sell us one of those Kitchen Joy Tool things, then I don't want to hear no more blabber. This kid's yap is more lethal than the big earthquake out in San Francisco. Shut it up, please!"

"It can't be done," John said, walking up. "I've tried."

"It's *got* to be done," the dark-visaged, younger man, whimpered. "I just can't take it—"

"Can't take it?" Ferdinand postulated thoughtfully as though he had heard nothing of the arguments concerning him. "Spence Abercombe, first cousin to Pa's uncle George Peebles, once said those very words. 'I can't take it no more,' he says, an then he upped and took leave of—"

"You sure you won't change your mind?" Frank asked as he did his best to ignore the incessant verbosity coming from the young man who sat beside him.

"No thanks," John replied, grinning. "They're yours, now, and so's Ferd. Enjoy 'em all."

"I'll try. I'm just glad the kid's not going all the way to Los Angeles."

"Yeah, I'll bet you are. I've decided ol' Ferd there could talk the scab off the world's biggest blister."

Frank Burns grinned. "Or the hide off a full-grown cow. Do you reckon he gargles with that axle-grease these birds spoke of?"

"Likely. Was I you, I'd haul him all the way to Los Angeles, anyway. Stick him in the same berth with these two anarchists, and it'd be pure torture. Ten to one they'd break before the train got to Nephi. Good way to get information, wouldn't you think?"

"I would at that. Only since I'd have to be with 'em, I'd go just as nuts as they would. Besides, it'd be extremely cruel and inhumane treatment. Nope, even murderers I couldn't do that to.

"Be seein' you, John. Good day, ma'am."

"Luck, Frank."

"Be careful, Frank," Ruby chorused. "And good luck with your . . . project."

And so in the growing darkness of the evening storm, John Phips and Ruby Alder stood while the wagon creaked off down the slight hill. Then, arm-in-arm, they turned and made their way to the snow-dusted Oldsmobile, and within minutes they were made invisible with the darkness of the storm and the evening settling around them.

Chapter 23

"The saints be praised, me garjus Ruby lass, but 'tis nothin' but the pure luck o' the Irish and one flannel-mouthed, scrawny kid who kissed the Blarney stone, that I ain't arguin' with the divil this same minute."

John was driving the Oldsmobile, and though there was already more than two inches of snow on the ground, the automobile handled it well and moved steadily up the hill onto the Highland Bench.

"You . . . you were really going?"

"I couldn't see any other way. I'd missed the McNamara brothers, and I could see that my staying would do nothing but make life more and more miserable for you. Your son doesn't like me at all, and you don't exactly know what to do with me. For your sake, it seemed best to head over the mountain and be gone. Of course, I didn't know this storm would be hitting so hard."

"Johnny, you don't understand, do you. I love you, you silly old Irish-talking Englishman. Without you, my life would be meaningless. With you beside me, I can face about anything."

"Even Willy?"

"*Especially* Willy. Johnny, as soon as he understands, he'll be the best friend you ever had."

"Yes, but will he ever understand?"

"I don't even know that I do," Ruby stated quietly.

"Shure and it's a simple tale, lass. Ye can hear it an' ye want to, if yer not minded of boredom."

Ruby laughed. "I'm not, Johnny. Let's hear it."

"All right. In a nutshell, Frank Burns and I have been friends for

years and years. I happened to be working in Pennsylvania when the
Molly Maguires got so strong, and Frank contacted me. He was
working for the government, and he asked me to go underground for
him. I did, and learned a great deal about organized labor and the
men who wish to see it enforced.

"Ruby, the workers have a great many grievances, and organiz-
ing is one way to solve them. Unfortunately, some of the men who
lead these movements are seeking wealth and power, not the good of
the men they are supposed to represent. They resort to murder,
bombing, arson, kidnapping, and other such bullying tactics, using
force and fear not only to win their goals, but to force the common
workers to stand behind them."

"Joseph Smith," Ruby said softly, "was certainly right when he
declared that it was the nature and disposition of almost all men, as
soon as they got a little authority, to begin to exercise improper
dominion over the lives of others."

"That he was, Ruby. That he was. Anyway, after Pennsylvania
there were other trouble spots, and Frank and I were always in the
middle of them, working with another man named McParlan.
McParlan is now head of the Pinkertons, over in Denver; Frank
founded Burns Detective Agency and works in the open, and because
I am such an ordinary-appearing fellow, I have always been able to
go underground and get into the very middle of the unrest. That way
I've been able to tell who were the legitimate workers with honest
complaints, and who were the 'Big Bill Haywoods' of the trouble,
the men who were festering it for their own selfish gain."

"So you *were* all those places that Willy said you were?"

"Well, I don't know what places he told you, but over the years
I've certainly been here and there. There's a lot going on right now,
too. Frank and I have evidence of political corruption in San Francisco, kickback schemes in the railroad industry, land frauds in the
Northwest, embezzling schemes in some of the nations's most powerful banks, racial strife, white slavery right under the noses of the
administrators of the newly passed Mann Act, and on and on. Ruby,
it is all tied together, too. Sure those McNamara brothers bombed
Willy's office and the *Los Angeles Times,* but who did they work for?
Who is behind all this?"

Slowly Ruby shook her head.

"I don't know either, Ruby, but I can tell you that McParlan has picked up a couple of hot leads, which he passed on to us, and Frank Burns won't rest until he has unraveled the entire ugly mess. Our hope is that the McNamara brothers will open a few doors, letting us into their organization even further than I have been able to get."

"But won't they . . . those men who are behind all this, try to stop you? I mean, *all* who oppose them?"

"Of course they'll try. That's why Willy's office was bombed. Beyond that, they'll hire fancy lawyers like Clarence Darrow out of Chicago. He got Heywood off on a technicality up in Boise, and you can bet he'll be the one who represents the McNamara brothers. That's why Frank Burns needs to move fast. Only with mountains of absolute evidence will we be able to stop this chain of satanic corruption that seems to be sweeping the nation."

"And what . . . what about you, Johnny?"

"Me?" Johnny laughed quietly. "Ruby me lass, tonight yer Johnny lad has retired from the firm. From now on, all I want to do is chop yer wood and pester ye to death with the fixin' of yer fine and fancy meals."

"Johnny, are you *sure?*"

For a moment John was silent, and the only sound was the automobile moving through the new and still-falling snow.

"Ruby, like I told you earlier, I'm an old man, for I've let my dreams nearly die. But they aren't dead, and I've known that since the day your brother James first told me that you . . . well, that I might enjoy seeing you. Ruby me darlin', fer such time as I have left of this mortal probation, until the garjus sound of harps calls me home, I'd like to enjoy the pleasure of yer company and do me haythun best to make ye a happy woman."

"Then we'll have to start by convincing Willy of who you are."

"Can you do that, Ruby?"

"I think so. I can show him some things, and with what you and I have to tell him—"

"Faith, me garjus Ruby lass," Johnny interrupted, his eyes straining forward through the falling snow, "but it looks to Missus Phips's boy Johnny as though we've got the divil's own problem upon us now."

"What? But—"

"Ah, now, Ruby, and that crowd at your home makes things look blacker than an anarchist's heart!"

"My goodness! What on earth can it be?"

"The posse, lass, every spittin' one of 'em."

"But . . . but . . . Oh, Johnny, they're here for *you!*"

"Shure and I'm thinkin' you're right," John breathed.

"What will we do?"

"Well, Ruby my sweet, if they take me, I'll be fixed for a spell. There'll be no proof of my innocence forthcoming, not for at least a few days. You heard what Frank Burns had to say, and I don't blame him at all. Nor can I give out that information myself. What he has yet to do is too important.

"Captured, then, I'll likely spend some time in jail. And if Darrow does his usual work and the McNamaras go free, I just might swing for the murders of those folks in Los Angeles. The last's unlikely, but then a man never knows. And that's the bold truth of it, lass."

Slowly John braked the Oldsmobile to a stop, Ruby's home still a quarter of a mile away.

"What do you think?" he asked quietly.

"I think . . . I think it isn't fair," Ruby cried, tears starting in her eyes.

"Yer right, me sweet lass. 'Tis sad tidings, for shure."

"Johnny," Ruby suddenly declared, her voice firm with conviction even as her eyes dripped silent tears, "it will work out! Willy will learn who you really are. I'll convince him, and then everything will be fine. We'll be able to live here together. And as I have been happy, at least your last years will be happy ones. Johnny, I promise that you'll never be lonely again."

"And if it doesn't work out?" John asked wryly.

"Then we'll go away together."

"You'd . . . you'd leave with me, Ruby?"

"In a minute, Johnny. I mean it. You and I belong together, and I will stay with you forever."

John Phips sat silently, listening to the idling engine and the whistling of the wind. His eyes were wet, and Ruby wondered as he wiped at them with his gnarled old hands. She had never seen him weep, and she suddenly knew, as she watched him, that his heart had at last been given to her.

"Ruby, darling," he said then as he wiped his eyes a final time, "let's go meet the boys."

"No, Johnny, don't. The law in these parts has been a mighty uncertain thing, and I'm not convinced at all that it has changed. You wait out here. Hide somewhere, and I'll go in alone."

John Phips looked at the elderly woman at his side. "You're sure?" he asked.

"Very."

"All right, you go talk to them. Get rid of the posse, and maybe when you and Willy are alone, you'll be able to tell him. With all my heart I hope that you can, for I've never wanted anything so badly as I want this."

"I'll do it, Johnny. But . . . but what will I say to get rid of all those men? They will surely ask if I have seen you."

"That they will," John replied as he climbed out of the automobile. "And when they do, tell them that the last you saw of me, I was heading for Los Angeles. That should get rid of the marshals and their men."

"But I can't lie."

"Goodbye, Ruby me darlin'. Faith and it'll be a long walk, I'm a thinkin'. And only a fool would be tryin' it, too. Any sane man alive would be holed up in a nice warm barn on a night like this. But it's likely off to Los Angeles with the likes of me."

With a wink and a smile John turned and started walking southward into the falling snow, toward the distant city of Los Angeles, and Ruby, her heart in her throat, watched him go. Then, resolutely, she slid under the steering wheel and started the Oldsmobile to moving again. She was going to convince Willy of John Phips's innocence. Either that, or she and John Phips would go where no one would accuse them. The decision would be a simple one to make, and the next few minutes would determine it.

Day 7

Thursday
October 27, 1910

Chapter 24

"Johnny?"

"It . . . it's me," the old man whispered as he huddled outside Ruby's darkened door. "C-can I come in?"

Quickly Ruby opened her door, and with a painful groan, John arose and slipped silently inside.

"Are there still men out there?" Ruby asked as she closed and bolted the door.

"They left, finally," John replied as he drew the rocker toward the stove and sat down. "I g-guess it got too cold. I know it did for me."

"Oh, Johnny," Ruby moaned as she lighted the old lantern, "what in the world are we going to do?"

She turned then, and instantly wished that she hadn't, for John saw her tears and struggled back to his feet.

"Ruby, what is it?"

"Johnny, sit back down and let me fix you something warm to drink."

"All . . . all right. Are the windows covered?"

"Yes. And that's why I lighted the lantern. The light is too faint to be seen through my blinds."

Ruby then busied herself pouring milk into a pan and heating it, while John Phips sat silently beside her, trying to ease the cold out of his trembling body.

"Here," she said softly as she handed him a steaming glass, "this should help."

John took it, drank a little, sighed heavily, and gave Ruby a wink to show his gratitude. Ruby smiled in response and then turned slowly away.

"I reckon they wouldn't listen to you?" John asked then, his voice almost a whisper.

"No," Ruby replied, and with the word out, her tears started again. "Johnny," she cried as she buried her face in her hands, "doesn't it *ever* get any easier? Isn't the pain ever going to stop?"

"Brother Wells said it would," John answered as he stood again and came to her. "You remember that, don't you?"

"I . . . I remember."

"It will stop, Ruby me darlin' lass."

"Well, I wish it would hurry! I have waited so long."

"Even William wouldn't listen?" John asked then, changing the subject.

"No, he wouldn't. I've never seen him like this, Johnny. He loves people. He always has. But his mind is so set against you that I can't even talk to him. He isn't loud or angry. He's just . . . just, well, determined."

"If he wasn't a determined man, Ruby, he'd never have been able to accomplish all he has in his life."

"You . . . you always stick up for him, Johnny."

"Well, he's a good man. I could hardly do otherwise."

Carefully Ruby looked up into John Phips's eyes. "You know, don't you," she said quietly, her voice trembling a little. "About him and—"

"Yes," John responded as he turned back to his chair. "I know."

"How long have you known?"

"I don't know, Ruby. Maybe always. I guess, when you get right down to it, that was why I came from Los Angeles."

"It . . . it wasn't me?"

"No, not at first."

Ruby's gaze dropped to the floor. "S-somehow I understood that, Johnny. All along I knew that I'd had little or nothing to do with your coming."

"Ruby me darlin', I had no hope that you'd even talk to me. No hope at all. When you did, and when I sensed all those feelings between us, well, I don't recall ever being so happy. But I've certainly failed in protecting William. And so the greatest gain of my life has also become my greatest loss. It has surely been a mixed-up week, Ruby lass."

"So what do we do now, Johnny Phips?" Ruby asked, drying more tears from her face.

"Do? Well, we've a choice, you and I. We can stay here and take our chances with the law and your family; we can separate again and hope to meet in eternity; or we can go elsewhere and spend what life we have left, together."

"Do you have a preference, Johnny?"

John Phips grinned. "Aye, me garjus one, but it's the divil's own choice, too. Me heart says to grab ye and go, but me tired old head says it'd be cruel to take ye away from yer family, haythun son or no. To give ye the quickest and most peace, my head tells me that I'd better slip out that door yon and be gone with myself."

"That certainly seems most reasonable," Ruby agreed quietly. "Could you do it?"

"Faith, but ye've a black-hearted tongue, Ruby lass. What sort of haythun question is that?"

"A hopeful one. Johnny, could you walk out that door now and be forever gone?"

"No, Ruby," John answered quietly, "I couldn't."

Ruby smiled. "I'm glad to hear that, me sweet laddie-buck."

Surprised, John Phips looked up into Ruby's moist and glowing eyes.

"Johnny, I do not want to leave my family, for I love them more than I love life itself. But I feel the same about you. My family is grown—they have their own lives to live, and so do you and I."

"So whatever we do, then, we do together?"

"Absolutely!"

"Well, I still think that the best choice is to stay and trust the exigency of the law."

"No, Johnny, I don't think so. My heart is weak, and I couldn't stand the fear I'd feel by seeing you arrested and carted off to jail, even if it was only for a few days."

"But Ruby, that's hardly any time at all."

"Perhaps not, but you forget that I have lived through scenes of the most terrible miscarriages of justice. I watched my brother Jons's life destroyed because of wicked laws and officers who had no choice but to obey those laws. I saw poor Jons arrested and jailed for no reason other than that he was trying to live his religion, and I saw him rot in that jail for almost half a year before a hearing finally allowed him out on bail, giving him a chance to escape to California and the anonymity of being James Y. Johnson.

"I watched my own Henry Alder flee my home in the middle of the night, time after terrifying time, and me never knowing from one day to the next if I would ever see the poor man again. No, my dear Johnny Phips, that is not a choice for me. That is a clear decision. I will not stand by while you are jailed because you have done your best to prevent a terrible crime.

"Besides . . ." she concluded, her voice drifting off.

"Besides what?"

"Johnny, I simply *can't tell* Willy. I can't bear such pain!"

For a long moment John watched Ruby as she wept, and she knew that he was suffering every bit as deeply as she herself. They both hurt, they had both suffered for so long. But would it never end? Would it never stop?

Finally, John Phips dropped his gaze toward the floor.

"And so?" he asked softly.

"And so the choice that is left to us, Johnny, is to leave."

"Now?"

"Right now! This very night."

"It's mighty cold out there, Ruby."

"Well, it *has* stopped snowing, so likely the storm has passed. But storm or not, cold or not, that is my decision. Johnny Phips, I intend to spend the rest of my life at your side."

John Phips sighed. "Faith, Ruby me lass, but ye are a determined one. It's no wonder that William is the same. The poor lad had no choice in his life, no choice at all."

"I know that." Ruby smiled through her drying tears. "I've always known that. But neither, I think, do any of us; at least if we want to serve the Lord and live righteous lives. For fifty years I've tried to do that, Johnny, and I've a feeling that the Lord is about to reward me for it."

"Well, if this old man who sits at your stove is the reward, Ruby me lass, then ye've been sadly short-changed."

Ruby giggled like a little girl. "Likely," she agreed. "But it's too late to change my mind. I want to write Willy a note, and then I'll be ready."

John looked up. "Say, do you think I should write him a message, too?"

"Johnny, I think that would be wonderful."

"Well, lass, fetch us each a pen and paper, and let's be after it before the night grows any later."

And smiling, Ruby hastened to comply.

Chapter 25

The pre-dawn night was cold and still when John rose from his writing and walked to Ruby's side.

"It looks cold out there," he said quietly. "Real cold."

"It does," Ruby agreed, "but the wind has stopped, and the snow, so I think the storm is over. These October storms look just awful, though they never have any teeth in them. Are you ready, Johnny?"

"The two valises are in the back seat of the Oldsmobile. Doesn't take a man like me very long to pack."

Ruby laughed. "I don't need much, either. I have my letter written to Willy. We can pack these quilts around us for warmth, and that should do it."

"Did you make these yourself?" John asked, admiring the fine stitching in the quilts.

"I did."

"You do beautiful work, Ruby. I've never seen better, especially this yellow star quilt. They look real warm, too."

"Thank you."

"Ruby . . . I don't know whether to leave my note to Willy or not."

"Why not?" Ruby asked, puzzled.

"I don't know. I just have a funny feeling about it. I think I'll take it along and mail it when we get to—"

"Don't say it, sweetheart. The walls have ears, you know."

John laughed. "All right, I won't. But I think I'll mail it from there."

The clock struck five, and in the light from the solitary lantern, John and Ruby looked at each other.

"Are you sure you want to do this?" John asked quietly.

"More sure than I could ever say, Johnny. There isn't any other way left for us."

"I suppose you're right. I just wish you didn't have to leave your home and family."

"You forget, sweetheart. *You're* my family now."

"Yeah, I do forget. Well, me fair and garjus darlin', bundle up and let's get after it."

Blowing out the lantern and opening the door, they both gasped at the savage bite of the cold air. For an instant they hesitated on the back porch, wondering. But then, because each understood that a decision had been made, even long ago, and that there were no choices left to them, the couple took the quilts and Ruby's treasured teakwood box and made their way out to the automobile.

"Sure wish we had a team and wagon," John growled as he worked at the crank. "If this contraption breaks down or gets stuck in the snow, we'll be in serious trouble. I don't know the first thing about fixing it."

"Where's your faith, Johnny? We just need to pray ourselves across the dry farms to the railroad and everything will be fine. It's less than five miles. We'll get there without any trouble at all."

"I shurely hope so, me darlin'. Faith and I do."

Once the automobile was started, which because of the cold took several minutes, Ruby bundled up with her sweetheart. Then she watched with a feeling of trepidation as the darkened outline of her home receded into the darkness behind them.

The snow had fallen to the depth of six inches, with small drifts here and there that were much deeper. By the time the laboring Oldsmobile Special had inched its way westward, down into and then up out of the bottom of the deep wash known as Dry Creek and onto the gently rolling land that stretched westward to the railroad, John and Ruby knew they were in for a battle.

The road was difficult because of the snow, almost impossible, and John was straining every inch of the way just to keep the automobile on the road.

"Ruby me love," he muttered as he fought the vibrating steering wheel, "this is a bad trail, rougher than a polygamist's beard. And to tell you the truth, I'm worried."

"So am I, Johnny. But the Oldsmobile is doing fine, and that climb out of Dry Creek Wash is the worst part of the journey. We're already on top of it, so maybe things will be all right."

"I hope so, me darlin'. I just have a bad feeling. I'm not strong like I once was, and my leg is so game I can hardly use it."

"Stuff and nonsense, honey. You do just fine. You're just worried about me because I've become such a weak old sister."

"Well, I am at that. But Ruby, that sky looks bad. If the storm starts in again, we're likely to be in severe trouble."

"It won't, Johnny. These fall storms always pass quickly. We'll be fine. Three more miles and we'll be at the railroad, and then the elements can rage and conspire against us all they want. We'll be on our way to a land where the sun always shines, and where people in love never quarrel."

"I admire your optimism, Ruby. I surely do."

But as much as optimism usually counts in the lives of good people, on that day it came up to bat and went down swinging in the lives of Ruby Alder and John William Phips. Optimism was a strike-out all the way.

Forty minutes after they had left home, and less than a mile out of Dry Creek Wash and onto the dry farms, John Phips's worst fears were borne out. Blind and black and suffocating as the inside of a hard-tied gunnysack, the gale raged down off the top of Windy Ridge. All landmarks were lost within minutes, all human instincts confused and useless shortly thereafter. It was a ground-blizzard such as neither of the two had ever seen.

In spite of the unbelievable conditions, John managed to keep the open-topped Oldsmobile moving for another ten minutes. But then the sturdy automobile slammed into a six-foot drift that had been all but invisible until the moment of impact. And from that moment on, the motorcar went no further.

Within minutes, the engine compartment filled with drifting snow. Then the inside of the automobile began filling, and in her heart Ruby felt a terrible, sinking feeling of doom.

"Ruby, me darlin'," Johnny shouted into the wind, "we've got troubles, you and I."

"What . . . what are we going to do?"

"I don't know. Let's get down on the lee of this motorcar, get under these blankets, and make a decision. One thing's for certain—this outfit isn't going anywhere very soon."

Quickly the two climbed under the meager shelter of the motorcar, where the engine still radiated a little heat. Then they pulled their quilts in after them, wrapped themselves together, and did their best to protect each other from the cruelty of the wind.

But, as though conditions were not already bad enough, the elements became worse, unleashing their fury with unparalleled vengeance.

The winds struck with the nerve-shredding suddenness of a hysterical woman's scream, and then they didn't let up. Thirty seconds after the first shriek, the wind was shaking the open Oldsmobile like a winter-starved bear shakes a spring shoat by the neck.

For three straight hours John and Ruby huddled together, while outside the quilts there was nothing but wild, strangling wind. Then, about nine o'clock in the morning, with the two old people still welded by common insomnia beneath the motorcar in their darkened, quilt cocoon, the snow began again.

"W-well, *Wasiya* is h-howling today," John stammered through chattering teeth.

"W-Wasiya?" Ruby asked as she pressed her shaking body against the old man's frail form.

"S-Sioux winter giant, honey. The Indian b-blizzard god. Ruby, we're in trouble, and we're in trouble deep. It's light out, the storm is getting worse instead of better, and I don't see any alternative but to walk for it. Otherwise we'll never be found."

"No, J-Johnny. We're b-better off s-staying here. I heard Jacob Beck tell the s-story of one morning finding a strange mound of s-snow in the road near his home. Upon investigation he found a f-family who had been caught in one of these s-storms. They had turned their wagon upside down and had c-crawled under it, and for an entire night had weathered the b-blizzard. After he fed them a hearty breakfast they were f-fit as f-fiddles and went their way."

"Ruby, we c-can't turn your Oldsmobile upside down."

"M-maybe not, but we surely can't go out in that."

"Not *we,* Ruby. Me."

"No, sir, John Phips. You w-walk and I'll be right in your tracks. We're in this together; we'll g-get out of it together."

In spite of their predicament, John grinned. "You'll d-do, Ruby lass. You'll do."

For an hour longer the two huddled together, praying and hoping that something would change. But if it did, it was only the degree of cold and misery they were feeling. That truly became worse. Finally, obviously unable to bear the thoughts of doing nothing any longer, John shook the quilts and struggled out of them.

"S-so we're going?" Ruby asked.

"I think we'd better, Ruby. Otherwise we'll f-freeze right here. You ready?"

"Ready as I-I'll ever be."

Working the rest of the way out from beneath the storm-battered automobile, John stood up against the tearing wind and helped Ruby to her feet.

"I'll bet it's ten below, by holy Michal O'Murphy!" John shouted into the gale. "Shure, and it's the divil's own beauty of a drop for but the fourth week in October!"

"With the wind, it's likely c-colder than that," Ruby agreed, shouting hoarsely. "Which way sh-should we go?"

"Only one way *to* go, Ruby, We go back."

"But Johnny, they'll catch you! They'll c-catch you, sure."

"And we'll both be alive."

"I won't be, Johnny. If you're t-taken away from me again, I'll die."

"What are ye sayin', lass?"

"I'm s-saying the railroad's to the west, our freedom's to the west, and th-that's the way we've got to g-go. Besides, we're a lot closer to that railroad depot than we are to my home."

For a long moment John stood silently while the wind tore at him and the snow pelted his wrinkled face.

"Ye always were a stubborn one, lass," he finally declared. "But

I can see that ye're likely right, as well. If that's your wish, Ruby girl, then to the r-railroad we'll go."

Wrapping themselves in the snow-covered quilts, the two travelers broke their way through the giant snow drift that had stopped the Oldsmobile. And then they pushed westward against the fury of the storm. John took nothing with him but the woman he loved; but beneath her blanket, Ruby clutched her precious teakwood box of treasures.

For the better part of an hour they staggered forward, falling, rising, falling again. Their worn-out bodies, working feverishly, ached with the dull throb of bruised and battered muscle and bone. Yet somehow they were able, again and again, to get their hands under them and push themselves to their feet.

John, his one eye closed by the battering he had taken, and his other a mere slit for the same reason, pulled Ruby along, his exposed hand literally frozen to her blanket. His other hand, the one he felt and pawed his way forward with, was swollen out of shape and beaten so badly by the packed snow that it resembled an animal's withered claw.

Often the two stopped and gasped for breath, and yet just as often they pushed forward once more, the will to live strong within them.

Finally coming to the edge of a high, hard-packed drift, the two dragged themselves to the top. But then Ruby's legs gave way and she fell back, her chin hitting the ground so heavily that a thousand lights exploded in her brain. After a minute, however, she tried to climb the drift again, this time digging her fingers into the grainy snow and pulling herself upward.

Doing so took all the strength she had, and on the top of the drift she lay exhausted, her eyes almost shut, her ears barely able to hear Johnny's whispered words of encouragement.

"Johnny," she cried suddenly, "I-I'm going blind."

"So am I, R-Ruby me darlin'. It's the wind and the cold."

"Can . . . can you see anything at all?" she gasped.

"I can't. I'm blind as a weanling cave bat, Ruby. Worse, I don't know if these old legs can go much further."

"But we've . . . we've got to keep going, Johnny."

"I know, sweetheart. I know. Only . . . I can't see!"

The pure panic of John's blindness set him wild, then, and Ruby watched in amazement as John, growling with anger, dug at his eyes, scooped up fresh snow and scrubbed them out, beat them crazily with the heel of his knotted fists. But nothing happened. Not a glimmer broke through. Not a shadow or shape nor a sound of movement showed anywhere about him. It was true! He could not see!

But the terrible realization acted quickly as its own sedative, and within seconds John was sitting quietly again, holding tightly to Ruby's hand, thinking.

"Ruby," he spoke quietly, "th-this blindness isn't permanent. I had a puppy once that got k-kicked by a horse. It stumbled around for a week, blind as could be, before its sight came back. Then I heard about an Oglala Sioux brave who got lost in a blizzard. For f-five days he was lost, and when the camp found him he was walking in empty circles five hundred yards away, out of his head and stone-blind. Three days and he was good as new."

"So th-there's hope?"

"Not hardly; not unless we f-find some shelter. The way I see it, we've got less than that in hours, Ruby lass. The storm's too bad, and we've way too f-far to go. It looks bleak, mighty bleak."

Numbly Ruby absorbed what John had said. And he was right. She knew it, and she knew too that the only shelter between them and the railroad was in the lee of such drifts as the one behind which they crouched.

The cold of the snow and wind seeped into their very bones, and they sat huddled together, shaking uncontrollably. A drop of blood fell from John's nose, congealing instantly as a crimson spot on the snow. In John's blindness, however, he did not see it, and so Ruby didn't say anything.

Struggling desperately, John finally got his hands under him, growled at his own weakness, and then began to crawl. Ruby did her best to follow, and the two went perhaps a dozen feet before they collapsed again, almost simultaneously, into the white and blinding snow.

"R-Ruby," John gasped, working his body around toward the

woman whose very life depended on his own. "Ruby, me garjus d-darlin', our only hope is to hole up and pray. I'm down and dead as a swallowed mouse in a horned owl's belly, and I can go no further. Lass, I'm thinking yer not much . . . better off."

"Johnny, I c-can still crawl. See, I—"

And then Ruby cried out in pain.

"What is it, Ruby? *What is it?*"

"My . . . my leg, Johnny. I . . . I can't use it. For years it's been giving me fits, and n-now when I need it most, it's gone. Oh, Johnny . . ."

"W-well," he chattered as he settled back into the snow, "faith and we're shure a c-couple of stove-up old fogies, ain't we?"

Ruby, her lips cracked and bleeding, did her best to smile in return. "We are, Johnny. W-we surely are."

In silence, John gently pushed Ruby down into the snow beside him, and then he began to scoop snow up around her.

"Wh-what are you doing?"

"We'll hole up right here, Ruby. We've no ch-choice, so we'll hole up and pray. The good Lord is bound to send somebody along."

"But we'll f-freeze."

"Then like you said, we'll do it together. Here, you put my coat on, and we'll wrap ourselves around with both of these blankets. If I can get on top of you so that we can k-keep each other warm, why, we'll be fine."

Without protesting, Ruby accepted the instructions and burrowed deeper into the lee side of the drift. John, struggling out of his coat, wrapped it around her. Then he pulled the blankets over them both, tucked them under as best he could, and in their darkness snuggled up against her.

"I-I've been wanting to do th-this for an awful long time," he muttered.

"W-why didn't you s-say so?"

"Bashful, I reckon. Always h-have been."

"I don't c-care much for bashful fellows."

"Faith, and now I remember."

"Y-you do not."

"Do so. B-best of all, I recollect the night we first kissed, after that p-picnic down on Cedar Hill. It was you kissed me; d-do you remember?"

"I kissed you?" Ruby questioned. "Why, what an impertinant soul you are, Johnny Phips. D-don't you ever change?"

"There! You so m-much as admitted it. I'm glad you finally did. It'll be good for your soul."

The two lay silently then, each of their minds playing with things long past, as their bodies welcomed the warmth of each other.

"Well, me darlin'," John finally said, "you'll get used to my bashfulness, I promise. Given eternity, you're bound to."

There was another silence then beneath the quilts, a long silence broken only by the screeching of the wind and the ragged breathing of the elderly couple.

"J-Johnny, are . . . are you afraid to die?"

The silence lengthened, and Ruby wondered if John Phips had heard. Finally, however, he answered, his voice deep and rasping, and sounding very far away.

"Afraid, me lass? No . . . not anymore. Not now that I have found you and your love again."

"Does that really make a . . . a difference?"

"More than I c-can say. But still, long ago the Lord and I became friends, and many is the day when I have ached to end this mortal hour and greet him face-to-face. If today's to be the day for it, then I am content."

"That . . . that's w-wonderful, Johnny. I f-feel the same. Long ago I stopped carrying my burdens in my heart. But I've wondered, for so very long, when Brother Wells's promise would be fulfilled."

"You remember it too?"

"It . . . it's the only thing I *do* remember, Johnny. Do you realize that we've had another week together, just as he promised?"

"Well, the man *was* a prophet."

"Do . . . do you think that the end of this week signals the end of our lives, Johnny?"

"I don't know. Brother Wells never said that."

"But it might be that our deaths mark the final fulfillment of that promise."

John Phips was silent for a moment. Finally, with a twisted grin, he spoke.

"Should that be the case, Ruby me lass, your dreams of flying will come true. And you won't need a flying machine, either."

"Only if I go up, Johnny. What if I go down? What if I haven't . . . haven't fully repented?"

"You have, Ruby. We both have. And should we cross over that old river between this life and the next, me darlin', I can't imagine anyone I'd rather make the journey with."

"Oh, Johnny. Do you . . . really mean that?"

"All my life I've wanted to say those words. I th-thank God that I have found you, and that I can say them n-now."

"But . . . but what about all the th-things we were going to do?"

"Ah, Ruby, me lass. We'll do them. W-we have all of eternity stretching before us. You know, the only thing that has ever really mattered to me, in all my years of living, is that I find my way back to you. Now, at long and eternity-deep last, that for which I have sought and hungered above all else has been g-granted me. I have f-found the woman with whom I will share the brilliant fires and faraway nights of eternity, and . . . and with whom I will listen in the celestial springtime to the wild cry of the warm south wind as it sings to us the eternal song of love."

"K-kiss me, Johnny," Ruby whispered faintly. "Please hold me t-tight and kiss me."

And so, wrapped tightly in the arms of each other's eternal love, John Phips and Ruby Alder, together again at last, kissed each other . . . hello.

Epilogue

The afternoon sun streamed warmly through the window, and dust particles drifted aimlessly in and out of the shafts of light, dancing separately, lonely. The Regulator clock beat a steady cadence for the dust dance, and it was joined by the rapid dripping of water, muted through the thick walls of the home. The snow was melting fast, and by morning it would be gone, leaving miles of mud as the only testament of the snow's passing.

Will Alder sat silently in his mother's old horsehair rocker, aware of the dust and the sun and the clock and the dripping water, but moved by none of it. His wife, Flora, sat across from him, crocheting quietly, and Allyson was in the parlor, reading.

In his hand, Will held a hastily written note, penned by his mother, and though he had read it many times, he still could not understand. Yet even now, it dominated his thoughts.

What had possessed her? Why would a perfectly sensible woman go hightailing it off into a blizzard with a man like John Phips? It made no sense to him, and until it did, he wasn't about to let go of it.

And John Phips. Imagine that old man being an undercover detective. The wire from Burns Detective Agency had come early that morning, and Will still had a difficult time grasping its contents. Why, all along that old man had been trying to protect him. In spite of how badly he, Will Alder, had treated him, John Phips had gone quitely about his business, and in the end he had used his mother and even that screwy Ferdinand Burroughs to apprehend the anarchists.

To say that he felt silly would have been an understatement; to say that he felt terrible, now that they had found his mother and the old man, would have been even worse. Good grief! Why did men persist in making such fools of themselves? Why—

Footsteps in the doorway made him look up, and as the doctor came into the kitchen, Will rose to his feet.

"Well," the doctor said as he washed his hands, "I've done what I could. Now it's prayer time."

"Doc, will she . . . Is she . . ."

"Oh, your mother's fine, Will. By giving her his coat and snuggling down on top of her, that old man saved her life."

"I know, and I can hardly comprehend it. But after all, he dragged her out there—"

"Ruby wasn't dragged," Flora stated quietly, "and you know it, Will. Remember that letter, and the wire this morning. She went of her own free will, and she wanted to go."

"But *why*, Flora? Detective or not, I don't understand why she was so attracted to that man!"

"I don't know why either. But he was likable, and she had known him from a long time back. Maybe they were once in love."

"Mother and John Phips? Flora, that is preposterous. If it were so, I'd surely have heard about it."

"Maybe not," Allyson declared as she walked into the room. "I've had a couple of beaus that I won't ever tell *anybody* about."

"Allyson—"

"Well, I have! And just because Grandma is seventy and I'm not, doesn't change anything. She told me herself that age doesn't change how we feel about such things. I'll bet she and Johnny were sweethearts a long time ago, and—"

"Allyson," Will said quietly, "I don't think you should pursue that line of thought. We have no way of knowing anyway, and—"

"Why don't you ask her?" the doctor asked from the hallway.

Will Alder's head snapped up. "Ask her? You mean . . ."

The doctor grinned. "That's right. She's awake. But Will, she's weak, so don't talk for long."

"Willy?" Ruby gasped faintly as Will hurried in and sat down beside her on her bed. "Willy, is . . . is that you?"

"Mother," he cried. "It's me. *Yes!* And Flora and Allyson, too."

"Oh, Willy, take c-care of Johnny . . . He has been k-keeping me warm, and—"

"We know, Mother. And he's . . . he's being taken care of."

"Oh, thank the . . . the good Lord. He is s-such a good man."

"Here," the doctor interrupted. "Drink this, Mrs. Alder."

Straining, Ruby did her best to swallow the warm liquid.

"Mother," William asked as he took her frail and trembling hand into his own. "Where were you going? What—"

"Willy," she suddenly cried, her voice filled with understanding, "he's dead, isn't he."

"Mother, I don't think—"

"Willy . . . *tell me!*"

"No, Mother," William answered in the stillness of the storm-deadened October afternoon. "He isn't. But he's in a mighty bad way. He's in the other bedroom, and the doctor is doing all he can for him."

"Oh, Johnny!" Ruby wailed, turning away from her son. "N-not now! You c-can't leave me, not after all these years."

"Mother, you don't know how lucky we were to find you. Talk about a miracle! Another twenty or thirty minutes, and . . . and . . ."

"Mother, *why* did you do this?"

"You d-don't know, do you Willy. I . . . I've tried to tell you a dozen times, and at least a thousand times I was . . . afraid to."

"Tell me what, Mother? I always listen to you. I always do."

With fumbling, bandaged fingers, Ruby pulled open the lid of her teakwood box of treasures, a box that Will had placed beside her on the bed when she had been carried in. Carefully, then, she took out the photograph that lay at the very top.

"Will, this is a photograph of your father and me on the . . . the day we were . . . married."

"But . . . but that isn't Father."

"But it is, Willy. It *is!* We were sealed by Brother Daniel H. Wells in the Endowment House in . . . in Salt Lake City. The date was March 23, 1862."

"You mean—"

"Yes, Willy. John William Phips, the man who saved my life

this morning, is . . . is the man in the photograph. You see, he signed each of our names at the bottom. John and Ruby Phips. He . . . he is your *father,* my dear. H-he is the man whose name you were given."

"That man is my *father?*" William asked incredulously. "But . . . but why didn't you *tell* me, Mother?"

"Oh, Willy, how can I say it? I . . . I . . ."

"Never mind, Mother. Don't say anything now. Just rest, and we will—"

"No, Willy," Ruby insisted energetically. "I can't rest. Not . . . not yet! I must tell you, so . . . so that you will understand. Johnny and I were . . . we went to be sealed to each other . . . *unworthily!* We knew we shouldn't do that, only . . . only we were so afraid and so . . . ashamed.

"But that night, after we had been sealed, we talked all night . . . and in the morning we sought out Brother Wells and told him of . . . of our unworthiness.

"Willy, we should have gone to our bishop and *not* to Salt Lake City and the Endowment House, just like folks come to you now when they need to repent. But travel was so hard, and we had already made the tragic mistake of going all the way to Salt Lake City and getting married unworthily. So, because we could not live with what we had done, Brother Wells, who was serving as second counselor to President Young, told us we could work out our repentance through him."

Bishop William Alder sat stunned, his mind reeling with the import of what he was hearing.

"So you were *married* to Phips?" he declared. "And besides, you . . . you . . ."

"Brother Wells did not . . . chastise us, Willy," Ruby continued, interrrupting her son. "Instead, he sent us out . . . and he went . . . before the Lord. A little later he called us back and commended us on our desire to . . . to come true before God and gain a measure of integrity. And . . . and then he gave Johnny his mission call."

"But how could he do that? Such a thing is not right."

"I know, Willy. It does seem contrary to the way things are done nowadays, sending a man on a mission before he has been cleansed by a time of sorrow and repentance. But Brother Wells was a prophet, and he had the right to speak for the Lord. He told us that this was the best thing we could do, at least in *our* case. Johnny's mission was to carry messages east and then to do as the brethren there directed him.

"I cried," Ruby continued, her voice more quiet. "But Brother Wells explained that it was . . . the Lord's will that we be given a week together and then be separated for a time so that both Johnny and I could learn about laws, and about . . . service. We had been terribly selfish when we had both known better, and a separation was the best way for Johnny and me to learn how to think of others. Brother Wells told us it was the price we had to pay.

"But he promised us that if we would both be t-true and faithful, that when our repentance had been completed and the Lord had forgiven us, we could forgive ourselves and each other, and then we would be reunited forever, with our eternal sealing still intact. He even said that someday we would . . . have another week together, if we were both worthy."

Ruby grimaced then, as her eyes closed, a tear working itself down her cheek. Will found himself aching with loneliness and with understanding, for he was certain that if he had known—

"Five more days we had together," Ruby continued, her eyes again opening. "Five of the happiest . . . and saddest days in my entire life. It was on the last of those five days, my dear son, that you . . . that you came into . . . being. Somehow I knew the exact moment when it happened, and I was not wrong."

"But . . . but Mother, I . . ."

Ruby, holding her weak and shaking hand up against her son's arm, stopped him, and then she continued, her voice strangely not quivering.

"Johnny left on his mission, Willy, and oh how I wept. And then, just six weeks later, and after receiving only three letters from him, he vanished. I learned from him only this past week that he had been wounded and mistakenly taken prisoner by the Confederacy. But back then, I didn't have any idea what had happened to him.

"When . . . when he never returned, Mr. Alder approached me.

He knew I was with child, and he and his first wife offered me a home. More importantly . . . he offered to be . . . your father. By then, of course, word had come back that Johnny had been killed, and I was almost past the grief of it. From what Brother Wells had told us, I was . . . certain that Johnny's death must have been the Lord's will, part of the price we had to pay, and the fulfillment of Brother Wells's prophecy.

"Thinking of your approaching birth," she concluded, smiling weakly up into her son's eyes, "I accepted Mr. Alder's offer. Both of us, Willy, thought it best that you look upon him as your real father. Besides, I . . . I was *so* ashamed! And that's . . . that's why you were never told."

"But when I was grown, Mother? Why not then?"

"I . . . I don't know. Somehow it never seemed quite time. I was always going to tell you, but I was worried for Mr. Alder's feelings, and I *knew* how . . . how disappointed you would be in me.

"But Johnny Phips, your *f-father,* loved you, Willy. More than life itself, he loved you. And he was so proud of all you have become. In . . . in his coat is a letter he penned for you last night. We were going to mail it . . . later. I think . . . I think you will enjoy it."

Without reply, William Alder stood and walked to the other bedroom. There he reached into John Phips's coat and retrieved the folded letter. This he brought back to Ruby's room and carefully read, and then read again.

"Oh, Mother," he cried, his tears suddenly released from where they had been held for so very long. "Until today I . . . I didn't *know.* I didn't *understand.*"

"He knew that, Willy, and that is why—"

"Ruby, me lass?"

Spinning, William was shocked to see John Phips leaning against the doorjamb, his face looking rough and haggard.

"Mr. Phips—"

"Faith, lad, but ye look like ye have seen a ghost."

"Mr. Phips, Mother just told me. I didn't know, and—"

"Johnny," Ruby cried as she pulled off her quilts and staggered to his side. "Johnny William Phips, you get back in bed this instant!"

"In bed? But lass, I thought ye wanted to fly. Hadn't we ought to be about finding us one of those new-fangled flying machines?"

"This is no time to be funning us, Johnny Phips. Now back in bed with yer haythun soul! I won't have you—"

"Oh, yes ye will, me garjus, darlin' lass. Ye'll have me forever, I'm thinkin'."

"Yes, yes, of course," Ruby whispered as she drew within his arms.

"And you, Bishop? If you'll have me—"

"Us," Ruby corrected quickly.

"That's right. If William will have *us*—"

"Have you?" Will Alder declared as he dropped John's letter and strode toward them. "Have you? Just let me get my arms around both of you, and you'll know the answer to that. I'm famous for my bear hugs, and if one of them isn't large enough to encompass a mother *and* a father, then my name isn't Will Alder Phips."

And with that, Ruby's boy Willy took his parents in his arms and squeezed, while his wife and daughter stood beaming, ready to join in.

And thus Ruby's seven days, as they had been promised by a prophet of God some fifty years before, were again, happily and fruitfully, fulfilled.

Historical Note

While the preceding story is fictional, and is based at least in part upon a dream Brent had in the spring of 1986, much of what was written is actual history.

American Fork and Highland, Utah, were as they are described. The businesses were owned and operated by the people named in the story. Civic and Church leaders, with the exception of the fictitious Bishop Alder, served as stated. The Alpine Stake Tabernacle cornerstone was dedicated October 24, 1910, by Elder Orson F. Whitney. Telephone and power lines were strung throughout the city between 1888 and 1889. Water rights from the creek that issued from American Fork Canyon—rights divided between American Fork, Pleasant Grove, Lehi, and the latecomer, Highland City—were still being settled in 1910 by armed sheriff's posses, and in 1905 a franchise was granted to B. Mahler to operate an interurban railroad through the streets of American Fork City, though it was never built.

American Fork Canyon was the scene of virtually all the activity that Ruby related to John. Mines gave forth precious metals from 1870 onward, lumber was an important industry from even before that time, and grazing followed soon after. The cities of Deer Creek and Forest City flourished; and Grave Yard Flat, the building terraces, and the charcoal kilns at Forest City are still visible today.

George Tyng struck it rich in Miller Hill, and the story of his encounter with the General Authority is, at the very least, commonly known folklore.

The railroad out of the canyon ran daily for six years, carrying supplies and tourists into the canyon, and ore and tourists back out.

Today, over a hundred years after it was abandoned, the old railroad bed still crops up in places, and even forms a hill in Blaine's front yard.

On the national scene, Theodore Roosevelt was president of the United States, the Gibson girls drawn by Charles Dana Gibson were the models that all American girls tried to emulate, automobiles were available, and flying machines were just coming into their own. The offices of the *Los Angeles Times,* which opposed organized labor, were bombed October 1, 1910. The McNamara brothers were eventually arrested for the bombing, though the book's description of the Utah episode of their career is fictitious. Attorney Clarence Darrow did defend the brothers, and he would have gotten them off had it not been for the extensive investigative work of Detective Burns, founder of Burns Detective Agency. Because of the evidence Burns compiled in secret, the McNamara brothers, in the middle of their trial, confessed, and were sentenced accordingly. Burns went on to become, in 1921, head of the Federal Bureau of Investigation.

James Y. Johnson, the pigeon rancher in Los Angeles, was the authors' great-grandfather. At the time of this story, he was actually in Los Angeles running the huge pigeon ranch and going under his "Johnson" alias to avoid prosecution for polygamy. Wyatt Earp was also in Los Angeles at the time, and all details of his famous gunfight at the OK Corral, including time and date, are accurate according to the most current research.

Even the storm described in the story is historically correct, though it did not happen in 1910. According to meteorologist Mark Eubank of Weatherbank, Inc., in Salt Lake City, the storm swept out of the Gulf of Alaska and into Utah the week of October 23, 1984, dumping twenty-three inches of snow in various Utah County locations, including the Highland Bench, during one twenty-four-hour period.